BAND DIRECTOR'S CURRICULUM RESOURCE

Ready-to-Use Lessons & Worksheets for Teaching Music Theory

CONNIE M. ERICKSEN

PARKER PUBLISHING COMPANY
Paramus, NJ 07652

Library of Congress Cataloging-in-Publication Data

Ericksen, Connie M.
    Band director's curriculum resource : ready-to-use lessons and
worksheets for teaching music theory / Connie M. Ericksen.
        p.   cm.
    Includes bibliographical references.
    ISBN 0-13-792169-1 (alk. paper)
    1. Music—Theory—Instruction and study. 2. Band music—Analysis,
appreciation. 3. School music—Instruction and study. I. Title.
MT10.E75 1997
784.8'071'2—dc21

97-37694
CIP
MN

Printed in the United States of America

10   9   8   7   6   5   4

ISBN 0-13-792169-1

ATTENTION: CORPORATIONS AND SCHOOLS

Parker Publishing Company books are available at quantity discounts with bulk purchase
for educational, business, or sales promotional use. For information, please write to:
Prentice Hall Career & Personal Development Special Sales, 240 Frisch Court, Paramus,
NJ 07652. Please supply: title of book, ISBN number, quantity, how the book will be used,
date needed.

PARKER PUBLISHING COMPANY
Paramus, NJ 07652

On the World Wide Web at http://www.phdirect.com

ABOUT *BAND DIRECTOR'S CURRICULUM RESOURCE*

The purpose of this resource is to help junior and senior high school band directors who, though busy preparing ensembles for performance, want to teach their students *about* music as well as how to play music. Its primary objectives are as follows:

- To provide a sequenced plan of instruction covering the fundamental elements of music and their easy application to the literature being prepared for performance.
- To offer "ready made" lesson plans that can be easily found and presented with minimal "on the spot" preparation.
- To include, as part of each lesson plan, an assignment that gives students an opportunity to apply and solidify the concepts presented in the lesson.
- To give the director and students a grading criterion that takes into account the students' musical understanding as well as their playing proficiency.
- To improve the overall musicianship of each student and the performing class as a whole.
- To help students enrich their lives by experiencing the aesthetic nature of music.
- To prepare students with sufficient musical understanding for enrollment in college music courses.

Band Director's Curriculum Resource is organized into the following six units of study: Linear Pitch, Vertical Pitch, Acoustics, Form, Style, and Duration. Each unit presents a particular facet of music and explores its place in actual band literature. It includes a vocabulary list, a set of lesson plans with related group activities and worksheets to be completed in class or assigned as homework, and a unit quiz. Five appendices at the end of the book provide games and activities to supplement the concepts presented in the lesson plans, lists of literature and recordings representative of specific forms and stylistic periods, and a bibliography.

Each unit begins with a list of salient vocabulary words and an accompanying worksheet. The lists are not organized in a lesson plan format and are not designed to be presented as lessons. You may choose to pass out copies of the lists to students for reference, or simply integrate the terms throughout the unit. However, it is recommended that students complete the vocabulary worksheet as they would any other assignment in preparation for the unit quiz.

All lesson plans are organized according to the following format: (1) lesson objectives, (2) advanced preparation, (3) sequenced "concept statements," and (4) group activities. Lesson objectives simply define the purpose of the lesson. If you recognize that particular lesson objectives do not meet the needs of your students at that time, you will want to substitute another lesson. Lesson plans are arranged, however, to ensure that prerequisite concepts for each lesson have already been presented.

Concept statements are sequenced bits of information intended to present musical facts in a concise manner. The statements will often need to be supplemented with examples and demonstrations from the teacher. Some possible examples are given within the prepared statements, but the director must monitor the students' response and determine if further instruction is necessary.

When applicable, the group activities at the end of each lesson are suggested as a supplement to the lesson plan. Additional activities designed as games or requiring full class time may be found by title in Appendix 1, "Games and Activities." Also, many of the lesson plans require reference scores and recordings as examples of the concepts studied. Any characteristic work may be used, according to the discretion of the teacher, but the appendices provide titles of representative pieces.

The worksheets following each lesson plan may be used as in-class or take-home assignments. Each worksheet is designed to encourage students' creativity as well as their short-term recall and learning skills of sequencing, listening, and transferring. Most importantly, however, the assignments are designed to promote musical understanding. It is strongly recommended that you frequently reiterate the concepts of the lesson, demonstrate how the concepts are used in the worksheets, and then continue to point out the application of the concepts in subsequent musical experiences.

Some questions on the assignment sheets have several acceptable answers. In such cases, and to promote creativity, you will have to consider answers carefully to assure that the students have made proper application of the lesson concepts. Also, some lesson plans are followed by more than one assignment worksheet. You may choose to assign one, all, or parts of each to further the understanding and application of the concepts.

Depending on your students' previous experience, of course, some units and lessons in this resource may seem juvenile and others complex. You will want to modify the presentation of lesson concepts according to the needs of the class.

Connie M. Ericksen

ABOUT THE AUTHOR

Connie Madson Ericksen has nearly 20 years of music teaching experience with students of various ages and musical abilities. Currently, she teaches junior high school band as well as preschool music, and high school band, including assignments with concert, marching and pep bands, bagpipes, and percussion ensemble. She is also associate conductor of the Civic Chorale in her hometown of Payson, Utah.

Mrs. Ericksen holds her Bachelor's and Master's degrees from Utah State University and Brigham Young University, respectively, and is presently working toward Kodaly certification. She has received numerous awards and honors as drum major of her high school, university, and bagpipe bands, and serves on the Payson Scottish Festival Committee.

An active member of the Music Educators National Conference and the Utah Music Educators Association, Connie is married to Boyd Ericksen (also a junior high band director) and they have two sons.

CONTENTS

UNIT THREE: DURATION

UNIT FOUR: ACOUSTICS

UNIT FIVE: STYLE

UNIT SIX: FORM

ANSWER KEYS

APPENDICES

A Note to the Band Director

As band directors, each of us faces the continuing challenge of achieving and maintaining a balanced curriculum. Most of our instructional time in a band class is typically devoted to preparing literature for concert or contest, and attention is focused on developing playing technique and, possibly, artistry in performance. Preparing for performance is an important objective of the class, but achieving a balanced curriculum requires focusing some time on more enduring objectives such as developing musicianship and enhancing the quality of students' lives through their music experiences.

The importance of establishing long-term, "enduring" musical objectives is stressed by Bennett Reimer in his book *A Philosophy of Music Education.** According to Reimer, the music teaching process should include discussion of and experience with specific elements of music and their expressive character such as tempo, the tension/release aspects of phrasing, the motion implied by the combination of rhythmic sound and silence, and harmonic progression. These specific aesthetic qualities are analogous to, or expressive of, the rhythms of organic existence—the patterns of life. With the ultimate goal of enhancing the quality of the experience of life, the role of the music educator requires that he consciously guide students to a recognition of the aesthetic aspects of music and the possible relationship these aspects have to the students' personal lives. The director's role demands a great deal of sensitivity to music and students, as well as teaching expertise. It requires more than the typical rehearsal habits of honing technical skills and polishing ensemble sound.

Although instrumental organizations are usually well received and publicly supported, the practice of devoting the entire class period to music rehearsal continues to be scrutinized. A review of salient literature reveals much discussion regarding what constitutes music education and how, or if, the typical goals of performance contribute to it. The related educational issues have been characterized as "note versus rote," "teaching versus training," "entertainment versus understanding," and "musicians versus technicians." Although the literature includes some support for the notion that "performance education" is education enough, the majority of writing is critical of the typical performance class routine of devoting all instructional time to the preparation of music for concert or contest.

In addition to the articles and literature discussed above, many organizations and projects have been initiated to define the term "music education" and promote its place in the public schools. Examples include the Contemporary Music Project (CMP), the Yale Seminar, the Manhattanville Music Curriculum Program (MMCP), the Tanglewood Symposium, the Hawaii Music program and others. A review of all these efforts suggests that the term "music education" should be defined as the literal study of music, and it was determined that such study is not typically taking place. According to these efforts, "literal study of music" would imply that in response to the director's question, "What musical knowledge have the students accumulated during the countless hours spent in

---

*Bennett Reimer, *A Philosophy of Music Education*, 2nd ed., Contemporary Perspectives in Music Education Series (Paramus, N. J.: Prentice Hall, 1989).

music class rehearsal?" a graduating senior could demonstrate understanding of musical terms, briefly discuss prominent composers and style periods, and provide a general description of festival pieces in terms of tonality, meter, contour, rhythm and form. Without this basic familiarity with music elements it would be difficult to defend a performing class as a course in music education.

Another major concern expressed in the literature is that high school music students are not adequately prepared to continue music study in college. For the majority of high school students, graduation marks the end of their playing career and the end of their studies in music. There will always be some, however, who will continue participating in music during their college experience, playing in a university band, or taking music courses to enhance their enjoyment. College directors, attempting to deal with lack of experience, are forced to backtrack and explain the most fundamental aspects of music. The learning deficit becomes especially apparent in those students pursuing a music degree and enrolling in freshmen theory classes. Professors share the desire for increased musicianship so that incoming students will be better prepared for college courses. One dean of music states:

> College administrators in the field of music frequently are depressed by the vast number of applicants for admission who possess only a meager knowlege of music fundamentals. Despite considerable skill on a major instrument, the simplest elements of notation are often unknown. Drill, of course, is imperative before a beginning in theory can hope to get under way.*

In her article "Bridging the Gap: Preparing Students for College Music Theory," Judith Bowman states that 12 percent of entering students at the Eastman School of Music from 1972 to 1976 were placed in a remedial theory course. It should be noted that these students were among the most musically talented in the United States, but their public school experience had simply not prepared them in the fundamental elements of music beyond mere performance.**

As my research for this project began, it became evident to me that many music educators have felt the need for a prepared curriculum. Some of them have struggled in their own secondary school teaching situations and seen a need to enhance their band programs with new methods and materials. Others have viewed the need from a larger perspective and expressed concern with the more enduring effects of limited music training, such as poor preparation for college or professional music experience, inability to identify and define the elements of music expression and notation, and over-emphasis of performance experience. Concern was also expressed that students typically were not provided opportunities to enhance their personal lives through the "feeling" and "emotional" aspects of music. Some concerned musicians and music educators grouped together to initiate projects and programs such as Manhattanville

---

*Owen H. Reed, *A Workbook in the Fundamentals of Music* (Florida: Mills Music, Inc.), 1947.

**Judith Bowman, "Bridging the Gap: Preparing Students for College Music Theory." *Music Educators Journal* 73 (April 1987): 49-52.

Music Curriculum Program (MMCP), the Tanglewood Symposium, the Hawaii Music Program, Contemporary Music Project, (CMP) and others. Many of the suggestions expressed in the literature as a result of these efforts have been included in this instructional resource as well as lessons and activities originating from the author.

Unit One

LINEAR PITCH

Linear Pitch Vocabulary List

Linear Pitch Vocabulary Worksheet

Lesson One

To present bass and treble clefs, note names and placement on the staff, half-steps and whole-steps, sharps and flats.

Lesson Two

To present the pattern of a major diatonic scale and provide opportunities for students to write, play, listen to and identify incorrect notes or pitches of any major scale.

Lesson Three

(1) To present the concept of key signatures and its application to all major keys. (2) To present the order of sharps and flats as used in key signatures as well as the proper placement of the sharp/flat symbols in a key signature. (3) To present the "circle of fifths."

Lesson Four

To present the chromatic scale and the three forms of the minor scale: natural, harmonic, and melodic and the solfege for each.

Lesson Five

To define the term "relative keys," and determine minor key by relating to major key signatures.

Lesson Six

To present the concept of intervals, and the classification of intervals according to (1) number of note letter names from one note to the other (represented by a number), and (2) the number of semitones from one note to the other (expressed as "perfect," "major," "minor," "diminished," or "augmented").

Lesson Seven

To further the understanding of intervals by specifically describing the intervals of octaves, fifths, and fourths, and their characteristics as perfect, diminished or augmented.

Lesson Eight

To further the understanding of the intervals of a second, third, sixth, and seventh by describing their characteristics of major, minor, augmented, and diminished.

1

Lesson Nine

To present the concept of inversion as it applies to intervals.

Lesson Ten

(1) To present the concept of a phrase as a melodic structure with a cadence as an aural melodic pause (progressive cadence) or stop (final cadence). (2) To point out the use of phrase markings in written music and encourage a more musical performance of phrases by discussing ways to follow the sense of motion intended by a phrase.

Linear Pitch Unit Quiz

2

LINEAR PITCH
Vocabulary List

©1998 by Parker Publishing Company, Inc.

Atonality   The absence of tonality—without relationship to key, root, and so on.

Dominant   The fifth degree of the scale.

Enharmonic   Referring to tones which are the same, but are named differently.

Fifth   The fifth degree of a scale.

Flat   The sign (♭) that indicates a pitch one half-step lower than the written note it precedes.

Grace note   An ornamental note written and played just before the main note it precedes.

Key   A tonal system with seven notes in fixed relationship to a tonic note.

Major/Minor   Names assigned to scales of specific half-step and whole-step patterns. Also descriptive of intervals.

Melody   A group of notes that make a tune. Also, the principle focus of a composition as compared to harmony, countermelody and so on.

Natural   A note that is not altered by a sharp or flat. Also, the sign (♮) that cancels previous instruction to alter a note.

Scale   An arrangement of notes fitting a specific pattern.

Semitone   A half-step. The smallest interval in Western music.

Sharp   The sign (♯) that indicates the pitch one half-step higher than the written note it precedes.

Tonality   A system in which music is written in a scale, or key, with all pitches gravitating to one pitch—tonic.

Tonic   The most important pitch of a key, the one to which all others gravitate. The first note of a scale.

Name: _____

LINEAR PITCH
Vocabulary Worksheet

Part one: Identify the true statements with a "T" and the false statements with an "F."

_____ 1. A *semitone* is a small ornamental note written just before the tone to which it is slurred.

_____ 2. *Enharmonic* refers to the lack of tonality, or without relationship to key, root, tonic, and so on.

_____ 3. *Dominant* is the fifth degree of a scale.

_____ 4. *Key* is a tonal system that fixes tones in a dependent relationship to a root, or tonic note.

_____ 5. *Tonic* is the primary note of a key, the first note of a scale.

Part two: Complete the sentences with the most appropriate vocabulary word.

1. A series of notes, following a specific pattern of whole and half-steps is called a _____.

2. A _____ is a note that has not been altered by a sharp or flat. It also refers to a sign which cancels a previous sharp or flat.

Part three: Select the answer that best represents the relationship described.

1. A tonic to a scale is like:
   a. butter is to bread
   b. the letter "A" is to the alphabet
   c. a lightbulb is to a lamp

2. Major to minor is like:
   a. red is to pink
   b. string is to a kite
   c. a book is to a car

3. Flat to natural to sharp is like:
   a. basement is to ground floor to upstairs
   b. dough is to bread to crust
   c. dark is to light to brilliant

LINEAR PITCH

Lesson One

Lesson objectives: To present bass and treble clefs, note names and placement on the staff, half-steps and whole-steps, sharps and flats.

Advance preparation: Staff lines and replica of keyboard printed on the chalkboard or large chart. Staff paper for students.

Concept statements:

1. *Pitches* or *tones* are named for the first seven letters of the alphabet.

2. The *staff* consists of five stacked, horizontal lines and the four spaces between them.

3. The *treble clef* is used to indicate the pitches within the realm of the female voice and the range of instruments *generally* considered to be soprano or alto voices of the band, i.e., flute, clarinet, french horn, saxophone, oboe, piccolo and trumpet. (Usually the entire *family* of soprano and alto instruments is written in treble clef, e.g., bass clarinet, tenor and baritone saxophones, and so on).

4. The *bass clef* is used to indicate the pitches found within the realm of the adult male voice and the range of instruments *generally* considered to be tenor or bass voices of the band, i.e., trombone, baritone, bassoon, tuba, and timpani. (A baritone part may be written in the treble clef to facilate transferring from a trumpet part.)

5. *Ledger lines* are used to indicate notes above or below the staff.

6. Treble and bass clefs together form the *great* or *grand staff.*

7. *Interval* is the distance from one note to another.

8. A *half-step* is the smallest interval found on the piano keyboard. It is the distance from any white key to an adjacent black key, or from a white key to its adjacent white key if they are not separated by a black key. *Chromatic* is a word to describe half-steps.

9. A *whole-step* is made of two half-steps. On a piano keyboard, a whole-step is the distance from any white key to an adjacent white key unless the white keys are not separated by a black key (B-C, and E-F); also, any black key to a neighboring black key, unless the black keys are separated by more than one white key (E♭-G♭ and B♭-D♭).

10. A *sharp* (♯) indicates a tone one half-step higher than the tone to which it is attached. Example: C♯ means the tone one half-step higher than C.

11. A *flat* (♭) indicates a tone one half-step lower than the tone to which it is attatched. Example: G♭ means the tone one half-step lower than G.

12. When designating tones higher or lower than notated, or written tones, the sharp or flat sign is placed before the note. When signs are used in conjunction with letter names, they are placed after the letter name. In

both cases, the tone is referred to by letter name first, then by "sharp" or "flat."

EXAMPLE:

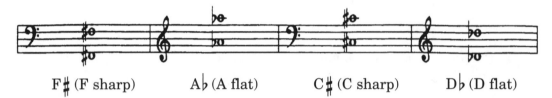

F♯ (F sharp)   A♭ (A flat)   C♯ (C sharp)   D♭ (D flat)

13. *Enharmonic* is a term used to describe an alternate name that can be used for any note name. Though the names are different, the notes are identical in pitch. Example: A♭ can also be called G♯, E♭ can also be called D♯, C♯ can also be called D♭, C♭ can also be called B, and so on.

14. When sharp or flat signs are placed next to notes they are referred to as *accidentals*.

Group activities:

1. Listen to, play, and sing half-steps and whole-steps up and down from any given pitch.

2. Select a piece of music from the band folder and identify ten examples of adjacent half-steps, and ten examples of adjacent whole steps.

Name: _____

LINEAR PITCH
Lesson One — Assignment One

Part one: Write the correct letter name of each pitch.

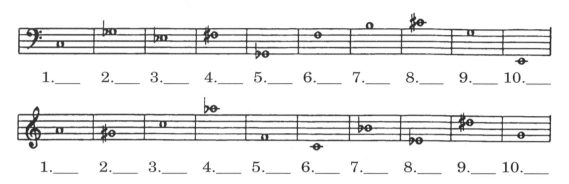

1.___ 2.___ 3.___ 4.___ 5.___ 6.___ 7.___ 8.___ 9.___ 10.___

1.___ 2.___ 3.___ 4.___ 5.___ 6.___ 7.___ 8.___ 9.___ 10.___

Part two: Fill in the blanks with the correct word to complete the sentence.

1. The _____ clef is used to identify the pitches within the realm of the adult male voice, and the range of instruments considered to be tenor and bass voices of the band.

2. The _____ clef is used to identify the pitches within the range of the female voice, and the range of instruments considered to be the soprano and alto voices of the band.

3. _____ is the distance from one pitch to another.

4. Notes placed above or below the staff are indicated by the use of _____ lines.

5. In order to indicate a pitch one half-step higher than the pitch given, a _____ is used.

Part three: Place a sharp sign (♯) or flat sign (♭) next to the given notes to designate pitches half-steps higher or lower as indicated by the arrows. Then write and name the enharmonic pitch.

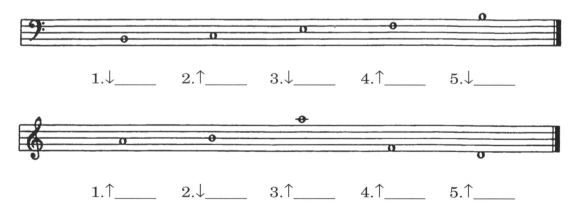

1.↓_____   2.↑_____   3.↓_____   4.↑_____   5.↓_____

1.↑_____   2.↓_____   3.↑_____   4.↑_____   5.↑_____

©1998 by Parker Publishing Company, Inc.

LINEAR PITCH

Lesson Two

Lesson objective: To present the pattern of a major diatonic scale and provide opportunities for students to write, play, listen to and identify incorrect notes or pitches of any major scale.

Advance preparation: Staff lines and replica of keyboard printed on chalkboard or large chart. Staff paper for students.

Concept statements:

1. A *scale* is a series or "ladder" of notes arranged to fit a pre-determined pattern of whole and half-steps.

2. The *major scale* is the most often used scale in tonal music. It consists of eight tones.

3. The first tone of the scale is called *tonic* and the eighth tone of the scale has the same letter name.

4. All adjacent intervals in the major scale are whole-steps except the intervals from tone three to tone four, and from tone seven to tone eight; these intervals are half-steps. The pattern of whole and half-steps of the major scale is as follows:

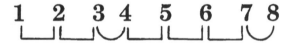

   (Eight tones—the first and the last have the same letter name. All adjacent intervals are whole-steps except three to four, and seven to eight.)

5. A major scale can be constructed starting from any tone as long as the pattern is applied correctly.

6. Starting on the tone (tonic) "C," the appropriate whole-step, half-step pattern of a major scale follows the natural sequence of the white piano keys. From any other tonic, the black piano keys must be used in order to construct a major scale.

7. In any major scale, all eight letter names must be used.

Group activities:

1. Listen to, play, and sing major scales beginning on various tonics.
2. Identify tones of a major scale that are played incorrectly and determine if they should be replaced by higher or lower tones.

Name: _____

LINEAR PITCH
Lesson Two — Assignment One

Part one: Write the pattern for major scales using numbers to represent the scale degrees; brackets (⌐) to represent whole-steps; and curves (◡) to represent half-steps.

Part two: Write the major scales in treble and bass clefs beginning on the tone indicated. Remember, use all the note letter names in each scale. If the interval between adjacent notes is too small or too large, use an accidental to adjust the higher note.

Tonic note

1. C

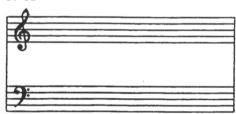

2. F

3. B♭

4. E♭

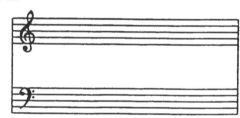

5. A♭

6. D♭

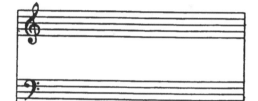

LINEAR PITCH, Lesson Two — Assignment One *(cont.)*

7. F♯

8. B

9. E

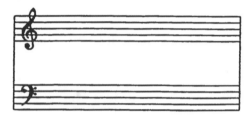

10. A

11. D

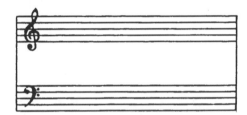

12. G

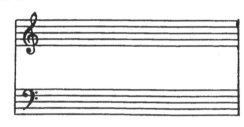

LINEAR PITCH

Lesson Three

Lesson objectives: (1) To present the concept of key signatures and its application to all major keys. (2) To present the order of sharps and flats as used in key signatures as well as the proper placement of the sharp/flat symbols in a key signature. (3) To present the "circle of fifths."

Advance preparation: Staff lines on the chalkboard or large chart.

Concept statements:

1. A *key signature* is used to indicate the sharps or flats needed to form a given scale. It takes the place of individual sharp and flat symbols placed before notes in a scale.

2. The sharp symbols (♯) are always placed on the staff in precise order and in precise places as follows:

    F, C, G, D, A, E, B

3. For key signatures using sharps, the last sharp (the one farthest to the right) represents the seventh scale degree. The tonic can be identified by counting up one half-step from this note.

4. The symbols for flats (♭), are always placed on the staff in precise order and in precise places as follows:

    B, E, A, D, G, C, F

11

5. For scales using flats, the last flat (the one farthest to the right), is the fourth step of the scale. The second to the last flat (the one second from the far right) is the tonic. Because the key signature for the F Major Scale has only one flat in its key signature, the tonic must be identified by counting down four letter names.

6. "C" is the tonic of a key signature with no sharp or flat symbols.

7. *"The Circle of Fifths"* is a system of arranging the major scales in order of increasing numbers of sharps and then decreasing numbers of flats (following the circle clockwise). It can be represented with a diagram:

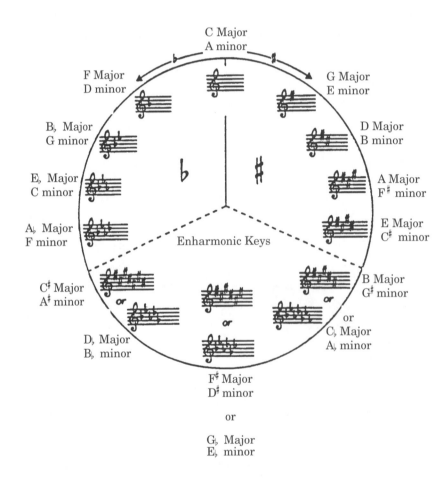

8. *Enharmonic keys* are those commonly called by either of two names.

Group activities:

1. Play the first five tones of the C major scale. Use the fifth scale degree to begin the G major scale. Play the first five tones and use the fifth to begin the D major scale. Play the first five tones… and so on, working clockwise around the circle of fifths and back to C.

2. Eventually learn all the major scales and play them completely working in clockwise order around the circle of fifths.

3. See *Keys and Key Signatures* (Appendix 1: "Games and Activities").

Name: _____

LINEAR PITCH
Lesson Three — Assignment One

Part one: Study the sharps and flats used in the following scales and write the correct key signature for each.

1.

2.

3.

4.

Part two: Identify the given key signatures and write and name the appropriate enharmonic key signatures.

1.

Key of_____
(flats)

Key of_____

2.

Key of_____
(sharps)

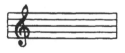

Key of_____

3.

**NOTICE
THE
CLEFS**

Key of_____
(sharps)

Key of_____

Part three: For each key indicated, write the appropriate key signature in both clefs.

1. B♭

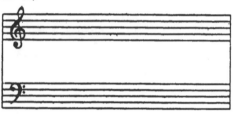

2. A

3. D

4. D♭

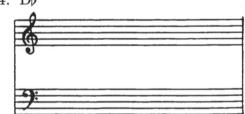

5. F

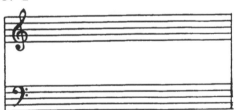

6. E♭

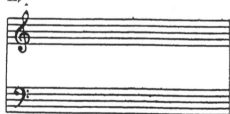

LINEAR PITCH, Lesson Three — Assignment One *(cont.)*

Part four: Identify the key signatures given.

1.

Key of _____

2.

Key of _____

3.

Key of _____

4.

Key of _____

5.

Key of _____

6.

Key of _____

Part five: Select any piece from your band folder and rewrite sixteen consecutive measures using accidentals to replace notes affected by the key signature.

©1998 by Parker Publishing Company, Inc.

15

LINEAR PITCH

Lesson Four

Lesson objective: To present the chromatic scale and the three forms of the minor scale: natural, harmonic, and melodic and the solfege for each.

Advance preparation: Staff lines and replica of keyboard printed on the chalkboard or large chart. Staff paper for students.

Concept statements:

1. The chromatic scale includes all of the twelve *semitones*, or half-steps, contained in an octave:

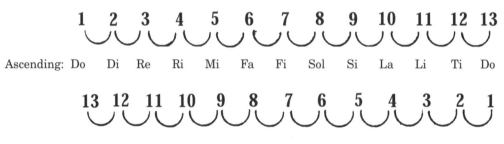

2. The chromatic scale can begin from any pitch and is named according to that first pitch, i.e., the "C" chromatic scale, the "F♯" chromatic scale, the "B♭" chromatic scale and so on.

3. The *minor scale* consists of eight tones, the first (tonic) and the eighth tone have the same letter name.

4. The minor scale has three different forms; each follows the same basic pattern, but varies slightly in the distance between steps 6, 7 and 8:

    Natural, or *pure minor:*

    All adjacent intervals are whole-steps, except between scale degrees 2 and 3, and 5 and 6.

Harmonic minor:

La Ti Do   Re Mi Fa   Si La

Raise the 7th degree one-half step which makes 6 to 7 three half-steps and 7 to 8 a half-step.

Melodic minor:

ascending

La Ti Do Re Mi Fi Si La

Raise the 6th and 7th degrees
one half-step.

descending

La Sol Fa Mi   Re Do Ti La

Just as the natural, or pure
minor.

5. All three forms of the minor scale can be shown together as follows:

Natural:

La Ti Do Re

Mi Fa   Sol   La

Harmonic:

SAME

5 6   #7 8

Mi Fa   Si La

Melodic:

SAME

ascending   *descending*

5   #6   #7 8   8   7   6 5

Mi   Fi   Si La La Sol Fa Mi

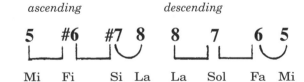

Name: _____

LINEAR PITCH
Lesson Four — Assignment One

Part one: Write all the notes of the natural minor scale using the given notes as "La." Then write the 5th through 8th steps of the harmonic and melodic (ascending and descending) minor scales.

Ab

Natural (first four notes)

Natural (last four notes)

SAME

Harmonic (last four notes)

Melodic ascending   descending

SAME

2. F

Natural (first four notes)

Natural (last four notes)

SAME

Harmonic (last four notes)

Melodic ascending   descending

SAME

©1998 by Parker Publishing Company, Inc.

3. D

Natural (first four notes)

Natural (last four notes)

𝄢

SAME

Harmonic (last four notes)

SAME

Melodic   ascending   descending

Part two: Write the chromatic scale in both clefs, ascending and descending, beginning from two different notes of your choice.

Part three: Beginning on any pitch, sing a chromatic scale with syllables and play the scale on your instrument.

Part four: Beginning on any pitch, sing the three forms of the minor scale in every key with syllables and play the scales on your instrument.

LINEAR PITCH

Lesson Five

Lesson objective: To define the term "relative keys," and determine minor key by relating to major key signatures.

Advance preparation: Staff lines printed on the chalkboard, or large chart. Also, charts printed with all key signatures.

Concept statements:

1. Each major key signature is also used to represent a relative minor key.

2. Two keys which use the same key signature are called *relative keys*.

3. The tonic of a minor scale is the step called "la," below the tonic of a given major scale. Therefore, to find the tonic, or name of a relative minor key signature, sing down from the major key—"do, ti, la." The minor scale tonic is "la." The natural minor scale results from following the whole-step, half-step pattern formed by continuing up the scale: "la" to "la."

EXAMPLE:

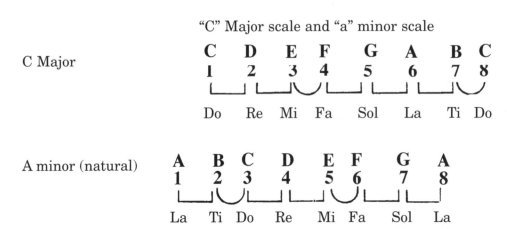

4. The same process is applied to key signature. Identify the tonic of the major key represented then sing down—"do, ti, la." The key signature remains the same, but represents a minor key and a tonic different than the major key.

EXAMPLE:

Key of E♭ Major . . . . . or . . . . . . Key of C minor.

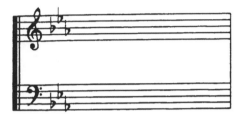

E♭ = **Do**, or tonic.   C = **La**, or tonic.

Group activities:

1. Find the relative minor scales to all of the major scales, using the method described.

2. Determine the relative minor key of all major key signatures.

Name: _____

LINEAR PITCH
Lesson Five — Assignment One

Part one: Identify the major and relative minor key.

1.   2.   3.

      (staff with treble clef and key signature)

Key of   Key of   Key of

_____ Major   _____ Major   _____ Major

_____ minor   _____ minor   _____ minor

4.   5.   6.

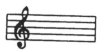      

Key of   Key of   Key of

_____ Major   _____ Major   _____ Major

_____ minor   _____ minor   _____ minor

Part two: For each of the major scales given, write the letter names and whole-step, half-step indications of the relative minor scale.

1.
Major:
E♭ F G A♭ B♭ C D E♭

minor:

2.
Major:
E F♯ G♯ A B C♯ D♯ E

minor:

3.
Major:
A♭ B♭ C D♭ E♭ F G A♭

minor:

4.
Major:
B C♯ D♯ E F♯ G♯ A♯ B

minor:

5.
Major:
D♭ E♭ F G♭ A♭ B♭ C D♭

minor:

6.
Major:
F♯ G♯ A♯ B C♯ D♯ E♯ F♯

minor:

Part three: Select three pieces from your band folder and identify the key signatures as possible major and relative minor. After playing through your part, identify which key is actually used—major or minor.

Title of piece	Major and relative minor key	Key actually used
1.		
2.		
3.		

LINEAR PITCH

Lesson Six

Lesson objective: To present the concept of intervals, and the classification of intervals according to (1) number of note letter names from one note to the other (represented by a number), and (2) the number of semitones from one note to the other (expressed as "perfect," "major," "minor," "diminished," or "augmented").

Advance preparation: Staff lines and replica of keyboard printed on the chalkboard or large chart. Staff paper for students. **After** the concept of intervals has been thoroughly discussed, it may be helpful to provide a copy or chart of the following table:

	Dimin.	**Minor**	**Perfect**	**Major**	**Augmented**
Second	C♯-D♭ (0)	C-D♭ (1)	——	C-D (2)	C-D♯ (3)
Third	C♯-E♭ (2)	C-E♭ (3)	——	C-E (4)	C-E♯ (5)
Sixth	C♯-A♭ (7)	C-A♭ (8)	——	C-A (9)	C-A♯ (10)
Seventh	C♯-B♭ (9)	C-B♭ (10)	——	C-B (11)	C-B♯ (12)
Fourth	C♯-F (4)	——	C-F (5)	——	C-F♯ (6)
Fifth	C♯-G (6)	——	C-G (7)	——	C-G♯ (8)
Octave	C♯-C (11)	——	C-C (12)	——	C-C♯ (13)

Using the key of C for an example, the table shows the possible intervals from tonic to each of the other scale degrees. Each interval is categorized according to diatonic steps (two steps is a "second," three steps a "third," and so on), and interval quality (diminished, minor, perfect, major, and augmented) according to semitones from one note to another. The number of semitones is indicated by the number enclosed by parentheses.

Concept statements:

1. An *interval* is the distance from any given note to another.

2. Intervals are classified in two ways:

   a. by the number of note letter names included when counting from one note to another.

   b. by the titles *diminished, minor, perfect, major,* or *augmented* as determined by the number of semitones (half-steps) from one note to another.

3. To determine the numeric classification of an interval, the staff provides hints for quick calculation:

   Intervals of a *second* (2) are those with notes on a line and the adjacent space, or notes in a space and the adjacent line. A second spans two letter names:

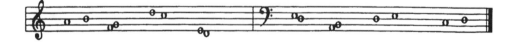

Intervals of a *third* (3) are those with notes on a line and the nearest line, or notes in a space and the nearest space. A third spans three letter names:

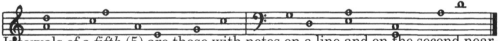

Intervals of a *fourth* (4) are those with notes on a line and in the second nearest space, or notes in a space and on the second nearest line. A fourth spans four letter names:

Intervals of a *fifth* (5) are those with notes on a line and on the second nearest line, or notes in a space and the second nearest space. A fifth spans five letter names:

Intervals of a *sixth* (6) are easily calculated by referring to the requirements of fifth and then going one line or one space beyond. A sixth spans six letter names:

Intervals of a *seventh* (7) are those with notes on a line and on the third nearest line, or notes in a space and the third nearest space. A seventh spans seven letter names:

Intervals of an *octave* (8) are those with notes on a line and in the fourth nearest space, or notes in a space and on the fourth nearest line. An octave spans eight letter names:

Group activities:

1. Select a piece of music from the band folder and identify various numeric intervals.

2. Practice writing various numeric intervals both up and down from a given note.

Name: _____

LINEAR PITCH
Lesson Six — Assignment One

Part one: Identify the following intervals as seconds (2); thirds (3); fourths (4); fifths (5); sixths (6); sevenths (7); or octaves (8).

1.   2.   3.   4.   5.   6.   7.   8.   9.   10.

11.   12.   13.   14.   15.   16.   17.   18.   19.   20.

Part two: Write notes on the staff above or below the given note (according to the direction of arrows) to form the interval indicated.

1. ↑5   2. ↓3   3. ↑4   4. ↓7   5. ↓6   6. ↑2

Part three: Write the letter name of the note above or below the given note (according to the direction of arrows) to form the interval indicated.

    A   G   F   C   D   B
1. ↓5   2. ↓3   3. ↑4   4. ↑2   5. ↓7   6. ↑6

©1998 by Parker Publishing Company, Inc.

LINEAR PITCH, Lesson Six — Assignment One *(cont.)*

Part four: Fill in the blanks to form true statements.

1. Besides the numerical definition, intervals are also described as _____, _____, _____, _____, or _____.

2. The numeric definition of an interval is determined by the number of note _____ names from one note to the other.

3. The number of _____, or half-steps from one note to another determines its non-numeric classification.

4. The numeric intervals represented by these pairs of notes are:
   B - D, _____;   C - G, _____;
   A - D, ` _____;   D♭ - E, _____.

LINEAR PITCH

Lesson Seven

Lesson objective: To further the understanding of intervals by specifically describing the intervals of octaves, fifths, and fourths, and their characteristics as perfect, diminished or augmented.

Advance preparation: Replica of keyboard. Staff lines on the chalkboard or large chart. Staff paper for students.

Concept statements:

1. A *perfect octave* (P8) spans eight letter names. It is the distance from any given note to the next note, either higher or lower, that has the same letter name. To be termed *perfect*, *both* letter names must be natural, sharp, or flat.

   EXAMPLE

2. A *perfect fifth* (P5) spans five letter names. With one exception, both letter names must be natural, sharp, or flat.

   EXAMPLE

   Because the interval between F and B has a unique combination of half-steps, a perfect fifth involving these letter names will *not* follow the rule of both names natural, sharp or flat. Memorize the exception for perfect fifths involving letter names F and B.

   Exception

3. A *perfect fourth* (P4) spans four letter names. With one exception, both letter names must be natural, sharp or flat.

   EXAMPLE

As with the perfect fifth, the exception for perfect fourths involves the letter names F and B. Memorize the exception for perfect fourths involving letter names F and B.

Exception

4. To be identified as an octave, fifth or fourth, the span of letter names must be eight, five, and four respectively. If a perfect interval is reduced by a half-step (either raising the lower note a semitone, or lowering the upper note a semitone) it becomes *diminished*. If a perfect interval is expanded by a half-step (either raising the upper note a semitone, or lowering the lower note a semitone), it becomes *augmented*.

EXAMPLE

Perfect and diminished intervals.

Perfect and augmented intervals.

Group activities:

1. Look for examples of adjacent intervals of fifths, fourths and octaves in your band music. Determine alterations necessary to create diminished and augmented from those perfect intervals identified.

2. Select a major scale and play tonic and the note a perfect fourth, then fifth and octave above it. Move to the second scale degree and play the note a perfect fourth, then fifth and octave above it. Continue through the scale, playing perfect fourths, fifths and octaves from each scale degree.

Name: _____

LINEAR PITCH
Lesson Seven — Assignment One

Part one: Identify all adjacent intervals that are perfect fifths, perfect octaves, or perfect fourths. Circle the two notes that form the interval, and write the name of the interval in the space provided.

— — — — — — — — — — — — — — — — — —

Part two: Identify the following intervals as perfect fifths (P5), fourths (P4), or octaves (P8); augmented fifths (+5), fourths (+4), or octaves (+8); or diminished fifths (°5), fourths (°4), or octaves (°8).

1. 2. 3. 4. 5. 6. 7. 8. 9. 10. 11. 12.

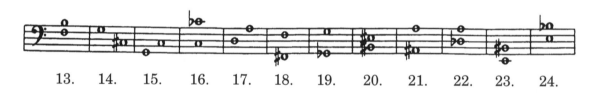

13. 14. 15. 16. 17. 18. 19. 20. 21. 22. 23. 24.

©1998 by Parker Publishing Company, Inc.

Part three: Using any music from your band folder, identify two examples each of adjacent fifths, fourths and octaves. Under the correct heading in the form below, write the name of the piece, the measure number, and the notes of each interval. Then, determine the alterations necessary to make each example fit its other two forms. Write the notes of the other two forms under their appropriate headings.

	PERFECT	**AUGMENT.**	**DIMIN.**
Example	"Theme from..." m. 13 B♭ - F	B♭ - F♯	B - F
Example	C - G	C♭ - G	"Suite of the..." m. 28 C♯ - G
Fifth			
Fifth			
Fourth			
Fourth			
Octave			
Octave			

Part four: Match the appropriate tune with the interval represented by the *first two notes.*

1.   Perfect fifth _____   2. Perfect fourth _____   3.   Perfect octave _____

    a. "Bali Hai"
    b. "Jingle Bells"
    c. "Here Comes the Bride"
    e. "Twinkle, Twinkle Little Star"
    f. "The Star Spangled Banner"
    g. "London Bridge Is Falling Down"

LINEAR PITCH

Lesson Eight

Lesson objective: To further the understanding of the intervals of a second, third, sixth, and seventh by describing their characteristics of major, minor, augmented, and diminished.

Advance preparation: Replica of the keyboard and staff on the board or a large chart. Staff paper for students.

Concept statements:

1. The interval of a second spans two letter names. A *major second* (M2), includes two semitones, or half-steps. A *minor second* (m2) spans two letter names, but includes only one semitone.

    EXAMPLE   Major seconds   minor seconds

    As you study the examples, refer to the notes on the keyboard. The intervals and their distinction as major and minor can be more easily understood by visualizing their relationships of black and white keys.

2. The interval of a third spans three letter names. A *major third* (M3) includes four semitones. A *minor third* (m3) includes three semitones.

    EXAMPLE   Major thirds   minor thirds

3. The interval of a sixth spans six letter names. A *major sixth* (M6) includes nine semitones. A *minor sixth* (m6) includes eight semitones.

    EXAMPLE   Major sixths   minor sixths

32

4. The interval of a seventh spans seven letter names. A *major seventh* (M7) includes eleven semitones. A *minor seventh* (m7) includes ten semitones.

    EXAMPLE   Major sevenths   minor sevenths

5. Any major interval can be made minor by reducing the interval by one semitone (without replacing either letter).

6. Any minor interval can be made diminished by reducing the interval by one semitone (without replacing either letter).

7. Any minor interval can be made major by increasing the interval by one semitone (without replacing either letter).

8. Any major interval can be made augmented by increasing the interval by one semitone (without replacing either letter).

    EXAMPLE   Diminished   minor   Major   Augmented

    Seconds

    Thirds

    Sixths

    Sevenths

9. As we *hear* intervals, we may think of them *enharmonically*. For example, playing the interval of a major second (M2)—C-D, *sounds* the same as playing the interval of a diminished third (° 3)—C-E♭♭. An augmented third (+3)—C-E♯, *sounds* the same as a perfect fourth (P4)—C-F. When identifying intervals *aurally* (by sound) it is more common to use the terms, major, minor, and perfect, than diminished and augmented. In writing, the specific numerical characteristics must be exact.

Group activities:

1. Find examples of seconds, thirds, sixths, and sevenths in your band music.

2. Practice playing the various intervals on your instrument. As you play, think of the intervals by two or three enharmonic names.

LINEAR PITCH
Lesson Eight — Assignment One

Part one: Write in notes, above or below given pitches (as directed by the arrows) to form the intervals indicated.

B. °3	m3	M3	+3

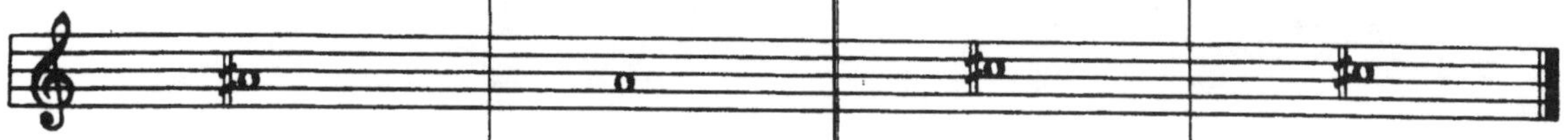

1. ↑	2. ↑	3. ↓	4. ↓

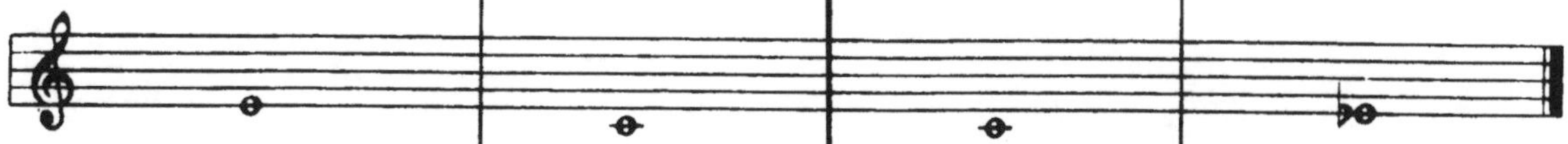

5. ↓	6. ↑	7. ↑	8. ↓

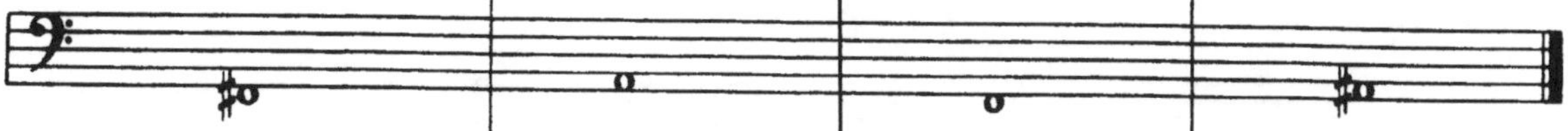

9. ↑	10. ↓	11. ↑	12. ↓

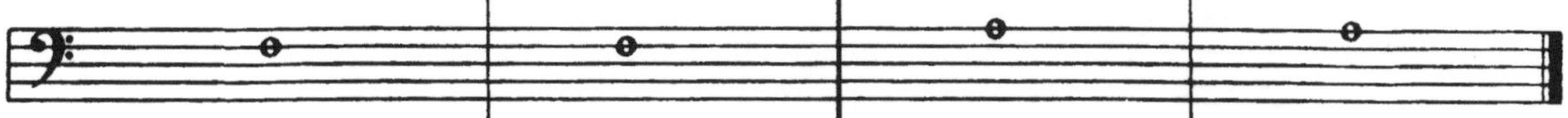

13. ↑	14. ↑	15. ↓	16. ↓

C. °6	m6	M6	+6

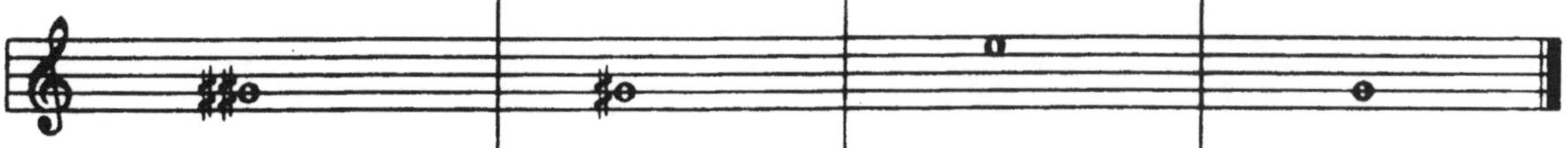

1. ↑	2. ↑	3. ↓	4. ↑

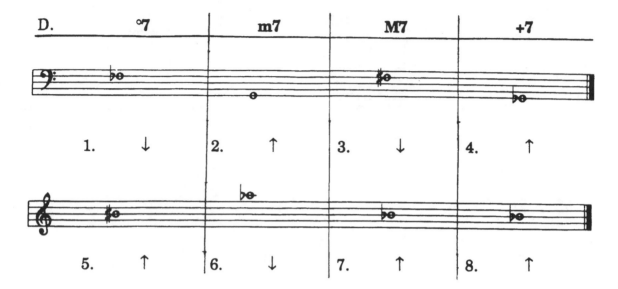

Part two: Identify the following intervals.

©1998 by Parker Publishing Company, Inc.

LINEAR PITCH

Lesson Nine

Lesson objective: To present the concept of inversion as it applies to intervals.

Advance preparation: Staff lines and a replica of the keyboard on the chalkboard or large chart. Staff paper for the students.

Concept statements:

1. Any interval may be inverted by transfering its lower pitch into the higher octave, or its higher pitch into the lower octave.

   EXAMPLE
   Intervals and their inversions

   M6   m3   P5   P4   M7   m2   m6   M3   m2   M7   m7   M2

2. By *inversion* a fourth changes into a fifth, a second into a seventh, a sixth into a third, and vice versa.

3. For intervals smaller than an octave, the sum of the numbers always equals nine; the sum of the semitones always equals twelve.

4. Both intervals together form an octave. Thus, a minor interval inverts to a major interval and vice versa. A diminished interval inverts to an augmented interval, and vice versa. A perfect interval inverts to a perfect interval.

5. An extension of the concept of interval inversion applies to melodies. When a group of intervals form a melody, the direction of each ascending interval can be changed to its corresponding descending interval and vice versa.

6. In *melodic inversion*, the size of the interval is not inverted, but only its direction. In this process, an ascending fifth becomes a descending fifth. A descending third becomes an ascending third. An ascending progression becomes a descending progression.

7. Melodic inversion is said to be *strict* if the original and inverted intervals contain the same number of semitones.

8. Melodic inversion is said to be *tonal* if the notes in the new direction utilize degrees of the scale in the appropriate key thus preserving the tonality.

EXAMPLE

Original sequence   Strict melodic inversion   Tonal melodic inversion

Group activities:

1. Practice inverting intervals and identifying them appropriately as major, minor and so on.

2. Select a short melodic passage from your band music and as a class, play through several measures, each person playing his part in strict and then tonal inversion. (Depending on the orchestration of the passage, a unison warm-up etude or scale exercise may be better.)

Name: _____

LINEAR PITCH
Lesson Nine — Assignment One

Part one: For each of the major, minor, and perfect intervals that follow, write in and correctly identify their inversions.

1. M3 _____   2. P5 _____   3. P4 _____   4. m2 _____   5. m6 _____

Part two: Use the given note as the bottom pitch of the interval named and the top note of its inversion. Write in notes to correctly form the intervals and correctly name the inversion.

1. P4 _____   2. °5 _____   3. +5 _____   4. m6 _____   5. M7 _____

6. °6 _____   7. M2 _____   8. m3 _____   9. P4 _____   10. +2 _____

11. m2 _____   12. m7 _____   13. +3 _____   14. °4 _____   15. M3 _____

LINEAR PITCH, Lesson Nine — Assignment One *(cont.)*

Part three: Rewrite the following melody in strict melodic inversion; then tonal melodic inversion.

1. Strict

2. Tonal

Part four: Select four pairs of adjacent notes from your band literature.
   a. Write the notes of each pair in the space provided.
   b. Identify the piece and measure number where each pair is found.
   c. Identify each pair according to the interval it forms.
   d. Write and identify the inversion of the original interval.

	Where Found	Name	Interval	Inversion	Inv. Name
1.	_____	_____			_____
2.	_____	_____			_____
3.	_____	_____			_____
4.	_____	_____			_____

©1998 by Parker Publishing Company, Inc.

LINEAR PITCH

Lesson Ten

Lesson objectives: (1) To present the concept of a phrase as a melodic structure with a cadence as an aural melodic pause (progressive cadence) or stop (final cadence). (2) To point out the use of phrase markings in written music and encourage a more musical performance of phrases by discussing ways to follow the sense of motion intended by a phrase.

Advance preparation: Students need their instruments during the lesson. The director must be prepared to play the chord progressions and melodic and rhythmic lines included with this lesson in order to demonstrate the sense of build and release inherent in phrases.

Concept statements:

1. A *phrase* represents a single musical thought and is comparable to a clause or sentence in prose.

2. The end of a phrase can be identified by the sensation of a melodic, harmonic, or rhythmic pause or stop.

3. Phrases are often indicated by the use of a curved line above the groups of notes included in any particular musical thought.

4. The points of pauses or stops are called *cadences*. Cadences can be compared to commas and periods in prose.

5. A cadence is labeled *progressive* if the sensation is one of pause only, and *final* if the sensation is one of stopping, or shutting off.

6. Within each phrase, there is a sense of motion which is always directed toward or away from a high point, or climax of the phrase. The high point may be suggested by the position of the cadence, the composition style, written accent, or changes in tempo, dynamic or rhythm.

7. Though the boundaries of a phrase may be indicated, the motion intended therein is not commonly indicated. The performer is responsible for expressing the sense of motion toward or away from the high point of the phrase.

8. A sense of motion may most easily be produced by the inflection of the four elements of musical sound—*duration, intensity, timbre,* and *pitch*. The sense of motion is most commonly achieved by an inflection of one or both of the first two elements; duration and intensity, or in other words, creating a slight change of tempo or dynamics.

Group activities:

1. Experiment with the melodies to determine phrase lengths, position and type of cadences, and expression of motion.

2. Practice playing familiar and memorized exercises while closely watching your director for conducted indications of phrasing.

LINEAR PITCH

Lesson Ten

Sample Chord Progressions, Melodic and Rhythmic Lines

Chord progressions—see appendix 2: Sample Chord Progressions

Melodic Lines

Tchaikovsky

Rhythmic Lines

42

Name: _____

LINEAR PITCH
Lesson Ten — Assignment One

Part one: Play each of the following melodies on your instrument. Then:

a.   At any point where you feel the musical thought pause, mark a "P" to represent a progressive cadence.

b.   At any point where the musical thought shuts off or stops, mark an "F" to represent a final cadence.

c.   Draw an arc over the notes included in each complete phrase.

d.   Indicate your sense of phrasing by marking the melodies with these symbols:

(crescendo symbol)	Gradually louder (crescendo)
(decrescendo symbol)	Gradually softer (decrescendo)
accel.	Speed up (accelerando)
rit.	Slow down (ritardando)
(staccato note)	Separate this note (staccato)
(tenuto note)	Lengthen this note (tenuto)
(fermata note)	Pause on or hold this note (fermata)
(accent note)	Louder on this note (accent)
(softer note)	Softer on this note

LINEAR PITCH, Lesson Ten — Assignment One *(cont.)*

1.

2.

3.

LINEAR PITCH, Lesson Ten — Assignment One *(cont.)*

Part two: Use the notes and note sequence of any three scales, but play each scale with the intent to express phrasing. Use any inflections of dynamics and durations (any rhythm you desire). Then write your versions of the scales using symbols presented above to represent your sense of motion.

1. Scale_____

2. Scale_____

3. Scale_____

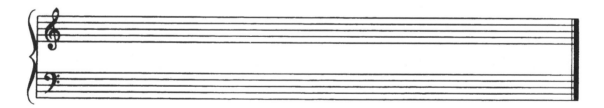

Name: _____

LINEAR PITCH
Unit Quiz

Part one: In the following melodies, write the letter name of each pitch. Then circle and identify any adjacent interval of P5, or P4.

1.

2.

Part two: For each of the following measures, identify the original key signature and, in the space provided, rewrite the measure in the new key as indicated.

1.

Key of _____   Key of B♭

2.

Key of _____   Key of A

LINEAR PITCH, Unit Quiz *(cont.)*

Part three: Write the Ab major scale first using accidentals, then with the correct key signature. Finally, write the relative minor scale (with key signature) in its three forms.

1. (Accidentals)

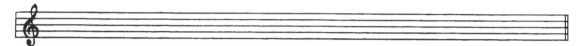

2. (Using key signature)

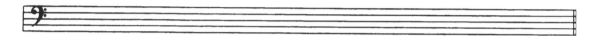

3. (Relative minor scale—three forms)

Natural   **Harmonic**   **Melodic**
All notes ascending   last four notes   last four notes ascending and descending

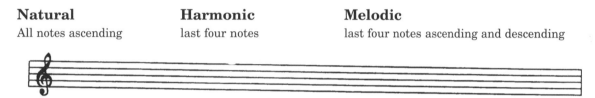

Part four: Write in the missing key signatures and then circle each note that should accordingly be played as a flat or sharp.

1. D Major   2. a minor

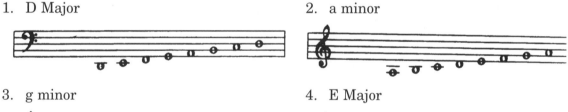

3. g minor   4. E Major

5. B Major   6. Db Major

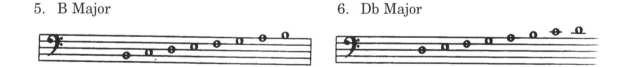

LINEAR PITCH, Unit Quiz *(cont.)*

Part five: Identify each bracketed pair of notes by its complete intervalic name.

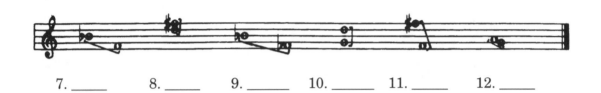

1. _____   2. _____   3. _____   4. _____   5. _____   6. _____

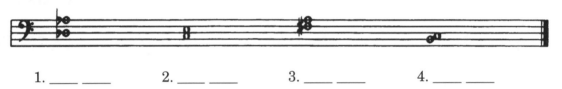

7. _____   8. _____   9. _____   10. _____   11. _____   12. _____

Part six: Invert the following intervals and correctly name the original and inverted intervals.

1. ___ ___   2. ___ ___   3. ___ ___   4. ___ ___

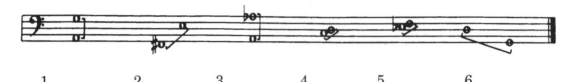

5. ___ ___   6. ___ ___   7. ___ ___   8. ___ ___

LINEAR PITCH, Unit Quiz *(cont.)*

Part seven: Draw an arc over each of the two phrases in the following melody. Identify each cadence as progressive or final. Rewrite the first phrase in strict melodic inversion and the second phrase in tonal melodic inversion.

Unit Two

VERTICAL PITCH

Vertical Pitch Vocabulary List

Vertical Pitch Vocabulary Worksheet

Lesson One

(1) To define harmony and introduce the concept of chords—specifically triads in root position and in the form of major or minor. (2) To define arpeggio and provide practice in writing and playing triads beginning from either root, third or fourth.

Lesson Two

(1) To present the characteristics of diminished and augmented triads. (2) To present the inversions of triads as 6/3 and 6/4 chords.

Lesson Three

To introduce the diatonic triads and basic chord progressions of the major and minor keys.

Lesson Four

(1) To introduce the term *cadence* as a way of describing points of musical pause or final rest. (2) To describe cadences generally as progressive or final, and then as authentic, plagal, half, or deceptive.

Vertical Pitch Unit Quiz

VERTICAL PITCH
Vocabulary List

Alto In four-part harmony, the voice or part second from the top.

Baritone A harmonic voice or part just above the bass when writing six parts, or the middle voice when writing for male trio.

Bass The lowest voice in part writing.

Cadence A melodic or harmonic formula that occurs at the end of a composition, section or phrase, and gives the impression of pause or conclusion.

Consonance Combinations of pitches that, in terms of traditional tonal music, provide momentary repose and do not require resolution to a different pitch combination.

Counterpoint The combination of two or more melodies sounding simultaneously.

Dissonance As compared to consonance, a note combination requiring resolution to a different combination in order to provide a more stable sound.

Harmony Simultaneously sounded pitches; the vertical element in musical texture.

Homophonic Music in which the melody is accompanied by only chordal accompaniment.

Mezzo Soprano Second highest voice part when written for six, or the middle part of a female trio.

Modulation Change of key within a composition.

Monophony Music of a single melodic line without accompaniment or additional parts.

Orchestration The art of assigning particular musical parts to specific instruments or voices.

Polyphony Music that simultaneously combines several melodic lines—of which counterpoint is a type.

Root The fundamental or generating note of a chord which may or may not be spelled in root position (with root on bottom).

Soprano The top voice in part writing.

Tenor The third to the lowest voice in six-part writing, or the second to lowest in four-part writing.

Texture The characteristic "thickness" of a composition. Texture is described by terms such as: thick or dense—many parts performing simultaneously, and thin or transparent—few parts performing simultaneously.

©1998 by Parker Publishing Company, Inc.

Third	The third scale degree, the interval of three whole steps, or the middle note of a root position triad.
Tonic	The first note of a scale or the chord built on the tonic note in a given key.
Triad	A three-note chord made of two stacked thirds.

Name: _____

VERTICAL PITCH
Vocabulary Worksheet

Part one: Identify each statement with a "T" for true and an "F" for false.

_____ 1. The *tonic* refers to the chord built on the first note of a scale.

_____ 2. A *triad* is a three-note chord.

_____ 3. The *tenor* is the highest written male voice.

_____ 4. "Polyphonic," "homophonic," and "thin" are all appropriate ways of describing *texture*.

_____ 5. The *alto* is the top voice in four-part writing.

_____ 6. *Harmony* is a single, unaccompanied musical line.

_____ 7. The *root* is the bottom note of a non-inverted chord.

_____ 8. *Orchestration* is accompanying a melody with chords.

Part two: Complete each sentence with the vocabulary word most appropriate.

1. One type of polyphony is _____.

2. The voice just below soprano in six-part writing is called _____.

Part three: Select the answer that best represents the relationship described.

1. Consonance to music is as:
   a. peanut butter and jam is to food
   b. the *Ford* brand is to cars
   c. heat is to ice

2. Modulation to music is as:
   a. oil is to painting
   b. changing lanes is to driving
   c. skipping is to running

©1998 by Parker Publishing Company, Inc.

VERTICAL PITCH

Lesson One

Lesson objectives: (1) To define harmony and introduce the concept of chords—specifically triads in root position and in the form of major or minor. (2) To define arpeggio and provide practice in writing and playing triads beginning from either root, third or fifth.

Advance preparation: Keyboard instrument to be used in demonstration. Staff lines and replica of keyboard on the chalkboard or large chart.

Concept statements:

1. *Harmony* results when combinations of vertical pitches are sounded together.
2. Certain combinations of vertical pitches are called *chords.*
3. In traditional *tonal* harmony, chords are made of tones arranged in thirds, beginning from the bottom or *root* note.
4. A three note chord is called a *triad*.
5. From the bottom up, triad notes are called *root* (1-do), *third* (3-mi), and *fifth* (5-sol).
6. Much like intervals, triads are specifically classified according to the number of semitones, or half-steps between pitches.
7. A *Major triad* consists of a major third interval (M3), from root to third (1-3), a minor third interval (m3), from third to fifth (3-5), and a perfect fifth interval (P5), from root to fifth (1-5).
8. A *minor triad* consists of a minor third interval (m3), from root to third (1-3), a major third interval (M3), from third to fifth (3-5), and a perfect fifth (P5), from root to fifth (1-5).
9. When playing on a mallet or stringed instrument, at the piano, or as a group, chord notes can be sounded together. Wind instruments individually cannot play an entire chord at once. Chord notes are often arranged to be played one after another and are called *arpeggios*.

Group activities:

1. Practice singing and playing pitches of major and minor triads when given one pitch as the root, third, or fifth.
2. Assign chord pitches to various sections or individuals. After sounding the chord, indentify each pitch as root, third or fifth.
3. Select chordal passages of music from your band folder. Identify each chord as major or minor. Practice identifying chord notes by requesting all those with the third to play alone, then those with the fifth, and so on.
4. Practice altering major chords by asking those who play the third to lower the pitch one half-step. Alter minor chords by raising the third.

Name: _____

VERTICAL PITCH
Lesson One — Assignment One

Part one: Fill in the blanks to make correct statements.

1. A three-note chord is called a _____.

2. In tonal harmony, chords are built in _____, beginning from the bottom or root note.

3. The top note of the triad is called the _____.

4. A broken chord is called an _____.

5. In both major and minor chords, the interval from the root to the fifth is _____.

Part two: Write three major triads for each given note using the note first as the root, then the third, and finally, the fifth of the chord.

    1.   2.   3.   4.   5.

    6.   7.   8.   9.   10.

    11.   12.   13.   14.   15.

VERTICAL PITCH, Lesson One — Assignment One *(cont.)*

Part three: Rewrite each major triad as a minor triad and each minor triad as a major triad. In each of the new triads, identify the bottom interval as a major or minor third as shown in the example.

EXAMPLE

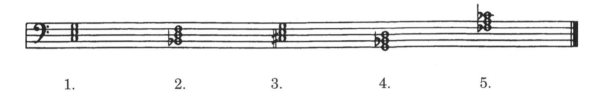

VERTICAL PITCH
Lesson Two

Lesson objective: (1) To present the characteristics of diminished and augmented triads. (2) To present the inversions of triads as 6/3 and 6/4 chords.

Advance preparation: Staff lines and a replica of the keyboard on the chalkboard or large chart. Students will need staff paper.

Concept statements:

1. Whether the quality of a triad is major, minor, augmented or diminished depends on the quality of the interval from which it is formed.

2. A *diminished triad* consists of a minor third from root to third (1-3), a minor triad from third to fifth (3-5), and a diminished fifth from root to fifth (1-5).

3. An *augmented triad* consists of a major third from root to third (1-3), a major third from third to fifth (3-5), and an augmented fifth from root to fifth (1-5).

    EXAMPLE

    Diminished triads   Augmented triads

4. Triads written with the root as the bottom note are said to be in *root position*. When the notes of the triad are maintained, but written (spelled) with the third or fifth on bottom, or in the *bass*, the chord is said to be *inverted*.

5. When the root note is written up an octave, the third of the chord becomes the bottom or bass note. The triad spelled in this way is in *first inversion* and called a *six-three* (6/3), or simply *six chord* (6). It is so named because of the interval from the bottom note to the top, and the bottom note to the middle (a sixth from bottom to top, and a third from bottom to middle).

6. When the root and the third are written up an octave, the fifth of the chord becomes the bottom or bass note. The triad spelled in this way is in *second inversion* and called a *six-four chord* (6/4). It is so named because of the interval from the bottom note to the top, and the bottom note to the middle (a sixth from bottom to top, and a fourth from bottom to middle).

EXAMPLE

Root position triads   First inversion   Second inversion

Group activities:

1. Assign members of the band to be "ones," "threes," or "fives," and have them play the root, third or fifth of a given major chord accordingly. Sound the chord, and use finger signals to first instruct the threes to move down by one half-step, thus forming a minor chord. Follow this process with various chords until students are familiar with the sound of major and minor triads.

2. Follow the instructions for the activity described above, but move the fives and threes so as to form diminished and augmented triads.

3. Write some of the triads played in the previous activities, and arrange the notes as chords in root position, first and second inversion.

Name: _____

VERTICAL PITCH
Lesson Two — Assignment One

Part one: Write the letter name of each chord and identify it as augmented (+), or diminished (°).

     1.   2.   3.   4.

Part two: Rewrite each root position chord as a $\frac{6}{3}$ (6), or $\frac{6}{4}$ inversion as indicated.

1. $\frac{6}{4}$ 2. $\frac{6}{3}$ (6)   3. $\frac{6}{3}$ (6)   4. $\frac{6}{4}$ 5. $\frac{6}{4}$

Part three: Next to each number, write the letter of the element needed to complete the given example.

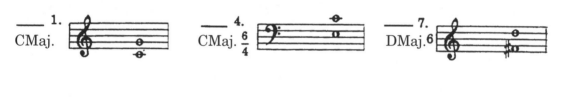

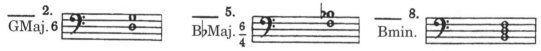

a. G natural   d. B natural   g. D natural

b. aug. fifth   e. E natural   h. ♭ (flat) next to E
     from 1 - 5.

c. dim. fifth   f. A natural   i. ♯ (sharp) next to F
     from 1 - 5.

VERTICAL PITCH
Lesson Three

Lesson objective: To introduce the diatonic triads and basic chord progressions of the major and minor keys.

Advance preparation: Staff lines on a large chart or on the chalkboard. Staff paper for students. The teacher should be prepared to play several basic chord progressions in various keys on the piano or assign a student to do so. (See Appendix 2: "Sample Chord Progressions.")

Concept statements:

1. Triads built on each degree of a scale are called *diatonic triads*.

2. Each diatonic triad is assigned a roman numeral and a name according to the scale degree of the root. Using C Major as an example, the triads, their assigned numerals and names are:

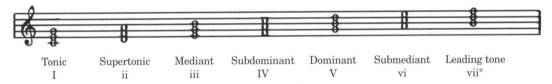

Tonic	Supertonic	Mediant	Subdominant	Dominant	Submediant	Leading tone
I	ii	iii	IV	V	vi	vii°

3. The simultaneous playing of chords and melody is called *harmony*.

4. In traditional harmony the most used triads of a major key are the I (tonic), the IV (subdominant), and the V (dominant). These are called the *primary triads*.

5. Together, the primary triads contain every tone of the major scale. For this reason they are frequently used in compositions and could provide a simple harmony for almost any melody.

6. The primary triads are important for establishing a feeling of tonality. The tonic (I) is heard as a point of stability—an "arrival" or resting chord. The subdominant (IV) is an intermediate goal—a digression from tonic that usually leads to the dominant. The dominant (V) represents momentum and typically leads to tonic.

7. The primary triads in minor keys are also the tonic, subdominant, and dominant.

8. In minor keys the tonic (i) and subdominant (iv) are minor chords. But an *accidental* must be used to raise the third of the dominant chord one half-step, thus causing it to be a major chord (V).

61

9. The third of the dominant chord is the seventh degree of the scale and is called the *leading tone*. The leading tone is an important element of the chord because it increases the sense of pull towards tonic.

10. Using the c harmonic scale as an example, the diatonic triads of the minor scale are:

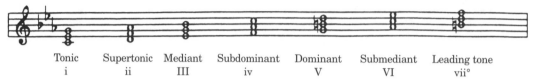

Tonic	Supertonic	Mediant	Subdominant	Dominant	Submediant	Leading tone
i	ii	III	iv	V	VI	vii°

11. The triad built on the seventh degree of the scale also includes the leading tone (seventh degree raised one half-step) and is, therefore, a diminished triad just as it is in major keys.

12. The non-primary triads of a key and inverted chord positions are used to make harmony more interesting in content and smoother in voice leading.

Group activities:

1. Assign the various pitches of the primary triads to class members. Using fingers to represent the tonic, subdominant and dominant chords, lead the class in playing through various chord progressions. Try the activity in several major and minor keys, emphasizing the use of the raised seventh degree or leading tone in the minor keys.

2. Extend the activity described above by memorizing a particular progression and then inviting an individual to improvise a melody with the chords.

3. Play arpeggiated chord progressions in unison. Experiment with various rhythms and meters.

4. Assign the notes of the non-primary triads and experiment with chord progressions substituting the II for I, the VI or III for IV, the VII for V, and so on.

Name: _____

VERTICAL PITCH
Lesson Three — Assignment One

Part one: Write the diatonic triads of the scales below. Remember to raise the seventh scale degree in the minor keys.

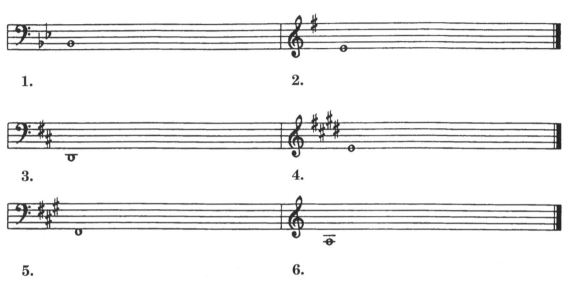

Part two: Play and memorize the following melody. Then harmonize the melody using the primary triads of your choice. Write the chords in the bottom staff and below each chord write its Roman numeral name. You may check your harmony by having someone arpeggiate your chords on *a like instrument* while you play the melody.

TREBLE CLEF INSTRUMENTS

BASS CLEF INSTRUMENTS

VERTICAL PITCH, Lesson Three — Assignment One *(cont.)*

Part three: Write a melody for the following minor chord progression (in the clef of your instrument or for the piano).

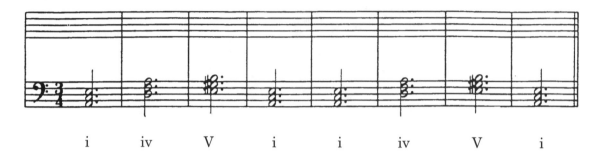

    i   iv   V   i   i   iv   V   i

Part four: Identify the chords used in the harmony of the following piece. Below each measure, write the chord names (such as E♭ Major, B♭ Major), and the Roman numeral symbols.

VERTICAL PITCH

Lesson Four

Lesson objectives: (1) To introduce the term *cadence* as a way of describing points of musical pause or final rest. (2) To describe cadences generally as progressive or final, and then as authentic, plagal, half, or deceptive.

Advance preparation: Staff paper for students and staff lines on a large chart or chalkboard. Someone prepared to play several simple pieces on the piano to demonstrate the aural sense of pauses and stops.

Concept statements:

1. In traditional western music, a *cadence* is a point of momentary pause or final rest.

2. Harmonic cadences are formed by two adjacent and different chords that end a phrase with a clear sense of tonality.

3. There are two general categories of harmonic cadences: *final* and *progressive*.

4. A final cadence is a point of obvious completion. Normally this cadence ends with the tonic triad to produce a sense of arrival.

5. A progressive cadence gives the aural sensation of a temporary stop or pause and usually ends on a triad *other* than tonic.

6. Within each category of cadences—final and progressive—there are more specific types of cadences.

7. Final cadences may either be *authentic*—motion from the dominant to tonic (V-I), or *plagal*—motion from subdominant to tonic (IV-I).

8. Progressive cadences include the *half cadence*—when the second chord is the dominant, and the *deceptive cadence*—usually motion from dominant to submediant, (V-vi).

EXAMPLE

FINAL CADENCES

authentic cadences   plagal cadences

V   I   V   i   IV   I   iv   i

PROGRESSIVE CADENCES

half cadences   deceptive cadences

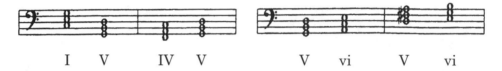

I   V   IV   V   V   vi   V   vi

Group activities:

1. Play chorale type exercises and ask students to momentarily put their horns down after playing a progressive cadence and to stand up after playing a final cadence.

2   Play chord progressions at the piano, stopping at various places and asking if the "passage" sounds complete.

3. Select sections of music from your band folder and ask small ensembles to play while other band members write measure numbers and indicate cadence points. Use the the letter "P" for progressive, and "F" for final.

4. When students become proficient at identifying general cadence categories, play various plagal, half and deceptive cadences and practice identifying each type.

Name: —————————————————————

VERTICAL PITCH

Lesson Four — Assignment One

Part one: Identify each chord with its Roman numeral symbol. Then at each cadence point mark "P" for progressive cadence and "F" for final cadence.

1.

2.

3.

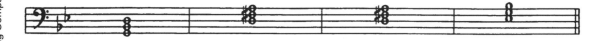

4.

5.

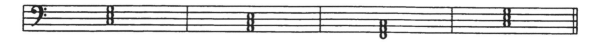

VERTICAL PITCH, Lesson Four — Assignment One *(cont.)*

Part two: First write in the bass clef key and meter signatures, then write chords above the Roman numerals to harmonize the melodies. Identify cadence points specifically: F a = final, authentic; F p = final, plagal; P h = progressive, half; P d = progressive, deceptive. Play through the melodies and arpeggiate the chords on your instrument or play melody and chords on the piano.

1.

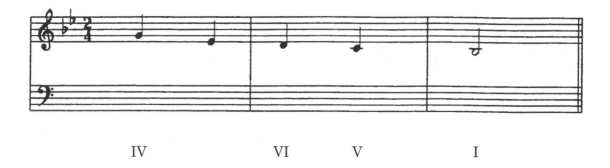

IV   VI   V   I

2.   Schumann

I   IV   V   IV   I   V

3.   Grieg

I   VI   I   IV   V   V   I   V

4.   Chopin

I   I   IV   IV   IV   I

5.   Mozart

I   vi   V   I   IV   V   vi

VERTICAL PITCH, Lesson Four — Assignment One *(cont.)*

6.

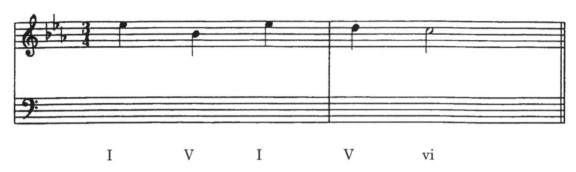

    I   V   I   V   vi

7.

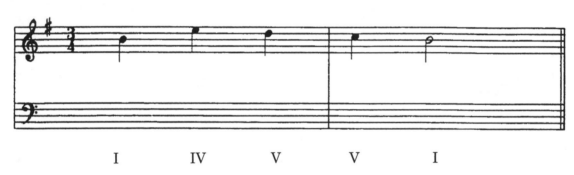

    I   IV   V   V   I

8.

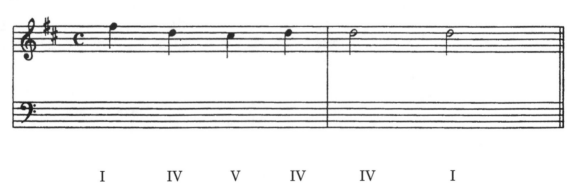

    I   IV   V   IV   IV   I

Name: _____

VERTICAL PITCH
Unit Quiz

Part one: Write the letter of the correct definition in the blank.

a. cadence   d. deceptive   g. mediant
b. triad   e. progression   h. diatonic
c. inversion   f. leading tone   i. dominant

_____ 1. A three-note chord built in thirds.

_____ 2. The only major chord in both the major and minor keys.

_____ 3. The III chord.

_____ 4. A group of notes played simultaneously.

_____ 5. A point of pause or stop in the music.

_____ 6. The movement of chords one to another.

_____ 7. A progressive cadence ending on vi.

_____ 8. Triads built from each tone of a scale.

_____ 9. In minor keys, the raised note of V.

Part two: Identify the chords as root position, first inversion ($\frac{6}{4}$), or second inversion ($\frac{6}{3}$).

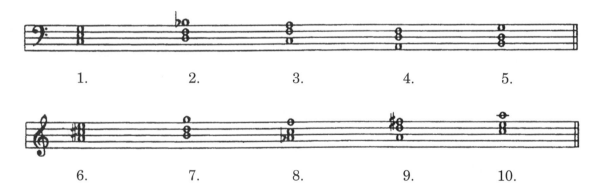

VERTICAL PITCH, Unit Quiz *(cont.)*

Part three: Identify the following chords with their letter names (EbM, D°, cm, etc.), and the Roman numeral symbols. Identify cadences as P=progressive, and F=final.

1.   2.   3.   4.

Part four: Write chords to form the indicated cadences.

FINAL CADENCES

authentic   plagal

1.   2.

3.   4.

PROGRESSIVE

half   deceptive

5.   6.

7.   8.

Unit Three

DURATION

Duration Vocabulary List

Duration Vocabulary Worksheet

Lesson One

    To define and explain the terms pulse, beat, accent, meter, measure, bar line, downbeat, stress pattern, and tempo.

Lesson Two

    (1) To present the musical symbols for various durations of sound and silence (notation). (2) To explain the function of meter indications (time signatures).

Lesson Three

    (1) To present the concept of rhythm, regular and irregular subdivisions, the terms beat, upbeat and offbeat. (2) To suggest the learning helps of foot tapping and note grouping.

Lesson Four

    To introduce the use of ties, dots and syncopation.

Lesson Five

    (1) To describe simple, compound and complex meters. (2) To introduce the terms triplet and duplet as ways of notating irregular subdivisions.

Lesson Six

    To introduce the concept of changing meters and the notation used to establish pulse from one meter to another.

Duration Unit Quiz

DURATION
Vocabulary List

Accent   Extra emphasis or weight on one note or beat.

Barline   A vertical line in music notation that divides one measure from another.

Beat   The steady, recurring *pulse* of music.

Complex Meter   Any meter wherein each pulse is not equidistant from the other pulses within the measure.

Compound Meter   Any meter wherein the pulse note value is divisible by three.

Count   The specific numeric name of each pulse or beat within a measure.

Cut Time   Another name for $\frac{2}{2}$ time (notated ¢).

Dot   In rhythmic notation, a mark following a note to increase its duration one half.

Downbeat   The first and strongest beat or pulse of a measure.

Measure   The space between two adjacent barlines.

Meter   The pattern of pulses and their accents.

Meter Signature   A notational device used to indicate meter—pulses within a measure and the pulse note value. Also called *time signature*.

Note Value   The duration of each note in relationship to the note assigned as the pulse value.

Polyrhythm   Simultaneous and contrasting rhythm in separate "voices" or lines of a composition.

Pulse   Steady, recurring units of time.

Rest   A notational device used to indicate different durations of silence.

Rhythm   Combinations of various durations of sound and silence.

Simple Meter   Any meter wherein the pulse note value is divisible by two.

Subdivide   To divide a pulse or note value into smaller units.

Syncopation   The irregular or unexpected occurrence of emphasis that causes a momentary contradiction of the prevailing meter.

Tempo   The speed of the pulse or beat of a composition.

Tie   A notational device used to combine the value of two adjacent notes.

Time Signature   Another name for meter signature.

Upbeat   The unit of time exactly between beats. Sometimes the unaccented beats of a measure.

Name: _____

DURATION
Vocabulary Worksheet

Part one: Identify the true statements with a "T" and the false statements with an "F."

_____ 1. *Pulse* is a series of steady, recurring, even, units of time.

_____ 2. *Cut time* is another name for $\frac{2}{2}$ time.

_____ 3. A notational symbol for silence is a *rest*.

_____ 4. *Polyrhythm* is any meter wherein the the pulse note is divisible by three.

_____ 5. *Complex meter* is any meter wherein each pulse is not equidistant from other pulses.

Part two: Complete the sentences with the vocabulary word most appropriate.

1. The speed of pulses or beats of a composition is the _____.

2. Each measure is bordered by a _____.

3. Combinations of sound and silence form _____.

4. Exactly between two beats there is an _____.

5. The value of a note can be increased by one half by placing a _____ after it.

6. The value of two notes can be combined by connecting them with a _____.

7. A pulse named by a number is called a _____.

8. Pulse note value and the number of pulses per measure is indicated by a _____ placed at the beginning of a composition.

9. A momentary contradiction of meter is called _____.

10. Counting "one e an da" for each quarter note pulse is an example of _____.

Part three: Select the answer that best represents the described relationship.

1. Simple meter is to compound meter like:
   a. four is to nine
   b. six is to twelve
   c. two is to six

2. Bar line is to downbeat like:
   a. "A" is to "B"
   b. blue is to aqua
   c. seven is to six

DURATION

Lesson One

Lesson objective: To define and explain the terms pulse, beat, accent, meter, measure, bar line, downbeat, stress pattern, and tempo.

Advance preparation: None.

Concept statements:

1. *Pulse*—often referred to as *beat*, is a series of continuous, steady, even, units of time.
2. The speed of pulses is called *tempo*.
3. *Accents* are strong or emphasized pulses.
4. When accents occur with regularity, pulses are grouped into predictable patterns called *stress patterns*.
5. Stress patterns usually are groups of twos, threes or their multiples. Pulses that have patterns are called *metric*.
6. Patterns of pulses are grouped into *measures*.
7. Each measure is separated from the next by a *bar line*.
8. The first pulse of each measure is the strongest and called the *downbeat*. In a conducting pattern, the first beat is identified by a downward motion.

EXAMPLE

Pulses and accent patterns grouped into measures and separated by bar lines.

> = strongly accented pulse; > = slightly accented pulse; ∪ = unaccented pulse.

DUPLE	> ∪ | > ∪ | > ∪ | > ∪ |
TRIPLE	> ∪ ∪ | > ∪ ∪ | > ∪ ∪ | > ∪ ∪ |
QUADRUPLE	> ∪ > ∪ | > ∪ > ∪ | > ∪ > ∪ | > ∪ > ∪ |
QUINTUPLE	> ∪ ∪ > ∪ | > ∪ ∪ > ∪ | or > ∪ > ∪ ∪ | > ∪ > ∪ ∪ |

Group activities:

1. Instruct each student to walk freely about the room at his own comfortable and even speed. Note the steady tempo of each individual as well as the variety of tempos throughout the room.
2. Play a recording of any music with a simple meter and steady tempo (a march would be ideal). Instruct the students to step to the pulse of the music. Eventually, have students identify the strong pulses by lightly clapping each.

Name: _____

DURATION
Lesson One—Assignment One

Part one: Use >, >, and ∪ to represent the stress patterns of the following texts. Write the pattern at least four times and use bar lines to divide the patterns into measures.

1. Mary had a little lamb, little lamb, little lamb.

2. Blueberry, apple and pumpkin pie too.

Part two: Fill in each measure with the appropriate symbols for accented, secondary accents, and unaccented pulses.

1. Triple meter—three pulses per measure.

2. Duple meter—two pulses per measure.

3. Quadruple meter—four pulses per measure.

4. Quintuple meter—five pulses per measure (arranged in twos and threes, or threes and twos).

©1998 by Parker Publishing Company, Inc.

77

DURATION, Lesson One—Assignment One *(cont.)*

Part three: Whistle, sing, or play the following tunes and indicate the meter and accent pattern of each.

1. "Yankee Doodle"

   Meter $\dfrac{\square}{\square}$

   Accent pattern

2. "America the Beautiful"

   Meter $\dfrac{\square}{\square}$

   Accent pattern

3. "Oh Susannah"

   Meter $\dfrac{\square}{\square}$

   Accent pattern

4. "Old McDonald Had a Farm"

   Meter $\dfrac{\square}{\square}$

   Accent pattern

Part four: Experiment with tempo by singing or playing the tunes in *part three* at different speeds.

DURATION

Lesson Two

Lesson objectives: (1) To present the musical symbols for various durations of sound and silence (notation). (2) To explain the function of meter indications (time signatures).

Advance preparation: Visual display of charts and tables used in the lesson. A metronome for demonstration.

Concept statements:

1. Pulses or divisions of pulses may be assigned sound or silence of different durations.

2. Various durations of sound are called *notes*.

3. Various durations of silence are called *rests*.

4. Notes and rests are named for their relationship to the whole note and whole rest.

5. The following chart illustrates the relationship between note values and rest values. The represented relationship remains constant regardless of tempo or meter:

sound—"notes"   silence—"rests"

whole note	whole rest
half note	half rest
quarter notes	quarter rests
eighth notes	eighth rests
sixteenth notes	sixteenth rests

6. A *meter indicator*—sometimes called simply *meter, time signature,* or *meter signature*—looks like a mathematical fraction and is placed at the beginning of each composition.

7. Meter indicators are used to (1) indicate the accent pattern of the composition—designated by the top number, and (2) to identify the note that is assigned to the pulse—designated by the bottom number.

8. Sometimes a meter indicator will be written with a number over a *note*, instead of another number like this: $\frac{2}{}$

9. Traditionally, in reading rhythms, each pulse in a measure is assigned a number and refered to as a *count*. Thus, the first pulse of a measure is count *one*, the second pulse is count *two*, and so on.

10. The duration value of notes and rests varies from meter to meter according to the specified pulse value as illustrated by the chart accompanying this lesson.

Group activities:

1. Write the following measures of rhythm on the chalkboard, then set a metronome at approximately 60 beats per minute. Ask students to clap the rhythms assigning a different note value as the pulse note each time (i.e., ♩ = 60, ♪ = 60, ♪ = 60).

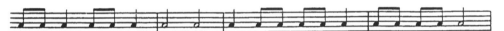

2. Select a piece of music from your band folder and practice counting the rhythms aloud—first in the actual meter, and then in a different, but related meter such as 2/2 for 4/4, or 3/4 for 6/8.

3. Write rhythms from various measures of a band piece on the chalkboard and ask students to replace selected notes with appropriate rests, or selected rests with appropriate notes.

DURATION VALUE OF NOTES AND RESTS IN VARIOUS METERS

some common meters	whole note	half note	quarter note	eighth note	sixteenth note
2/4 or 2/♩	NA	2 counts	1 count	1/2 count	1/4 count
counted		1 - 2	1-2-3-4	1+2+...	1e+a ...
3/4 or 3/♩	NA	2 counts	1 count	1/2 count	1/4 count
counted					
2/2 or 2/♩	2 counts	1 count	1/2 count	1/4 count	1/8 count
counted	1 - 2	1 2	1+2+	1e+a ...	
4/4 or 4/♩	4 counts	2 counts	1 count	1/2 count	1/4 count
counted	1-2-3-4	1-2 3-4	1-2-3-4	1+2+...	1e+a...
6/8 or 6/♪	NA	NA	2 counts	1 count	1/2 count
counted			1-2 3	1-2-3	1+2+
12/8 or 12/♪	NA	NA	2 counts	1 count	1/2 count
counted					
5/8 or 5/♪	NA	NA	2 counts	1 count	1/2 count
counted					
7/8 or 7/♪	NA	NA	2 counts	1 count	1/2 count
counted					

DURATION
Lesson Two—Assignment One

Part one: Fill in the blanks with the letter that most accurately pairs the given information.

1. 𝅗𝅥 ____	a. ♪ = 1 pulse
2. 𝄽 ____	b. 4 sound counts in $\frac{4}{4}$
3. ♫ ____	c. sound = 𝄽 (silence)
4. 𝄾 ____	d. in $\frac{2}{2}$, "1 e"
5. 6/8 ____	e. rest = 𝅝
6. 𝅝 ____	f. 𝅝 = 2 counts
7. 𝄻 ____	g. silence = 𝅘𝅥
8. 7/8 ____	h. subdivided = ♫
9. 𝅘𝅥𝅯𝅘𝅥𝅯𝅘𝅥𝅯𝅘𝅥𝅯 ____	i. 𝄻
10. 𝄾 ____	j. $\frac{2}{\circ}$
11. 2/2 ____	k. seven ♪s per measure
12. 𝅘𝅥 ____	l. rest = ♫𝅘𝅥 sound
13. 𝄻 𝄻 ____	m. silence = ♪ sound
14. 𝅗𝅥 = 𝅘𝅥 ____	n. pulse in $\frac{6}{8}$ and pulse in $\frac{3}{2}$
15. 𝅗𝅥· ____	o. is not used in $\frac{4}{4}$
16. 2/4 ____	p. 𝄼
17. 𝄽 + 𝄽 = ____	q. silence = 𝅘𝅥 ♪ sound
18. ♪ = 𝅗𝅥 ____	r. in $\frac{2}{2}$, one pulse
19. 𝄽 𝄾 ____	s. in $\frac{2}{2}$ and $\frac{2}{4}$
20. 𝄾 𝄾 ____	t. silence one half count in $\frac{6}{8}$

©1998 by Parker Publishing Company, Inc.

DURATION, Lesson Two—Assignment One *(cont.)*

Part two: Fill in the blanks to make correct statements.

1. A half note is equal to _____ eighth notes.

2. Three quarter rests are three times as long as _____ eighth rests.

3. A _____ in $\frac{4}{4}$ gets the same counts as two half notes in $\frac{4}{4}$.

4. _____ undotted quarter notes would fit in a $\frac{6}{8}$ measure.

5. One, but not two _____ would fit in a $\frac{5}{8}$ measure.

Part three: For each example, circle all notes assigned as the pulse note.

1.

2.

3.

DURATION

Lesson Three

Lesson objectives: (1) To present the concept of rhythm, regular and irregular subdivisions, the terms beat, upbeat and offbeat. (2) To suggest the learning helps of foot tapping and note grouping.

Advance preparation: The lesson involves much writing on the chalkboard but, because each concept builds on prior concepts, the writing cannot effectively be prepared beforehand.

Concept statements:

1. Various durations of sound and silence can be assigned to counts or portions of counts to form *rhythm*.

2. Rhythm patterns vary, but within each measure, the combined duration values of sound and silence must be equal to the number of counts designated by the meter signature.

3. In reading and writing rhythms, it is often helpful to consider one pulse at a time and to tap the foot on each pulse.

4. Since one pulse, beat, or count represents one unit of time, it can be divided into smaller portions of time. Dividing a unit of time is called *subdividing*.

5. When subdiving entire pulses, beats, or counts, it is helpful to represent the original, complete pulse as a circle.

EXAMPLE

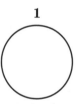

1

The circle represents:

> A half note if pulse note is the half.
> A quarter note if pulse note is the quarter.
> An eighth note if pulse note is the eighth.

6. A pulse can be divided into two equal halves. In counting, the first half is assigned a number and referred to as being *on the beat*. The second half is assigned the name *and*, and is referred to as being *off the beat* (*offbeat*), or being *on the upbeat* (*upbeat*). When tapping the foot, the toe hits the floor on the beat and is raised to its peak on the upbeat.

84

EXAMPLE

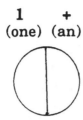

1   +
(one) (an)

7. A pulse can be further subdivided by splitting the beat and the upbeat
    into two equal parts. In counting, the names of the original halves
    remain the same, the new parts are called *e* and *da*. (Usually the subdi-
    vision is written *1 e an da*.)

EXAMPLE

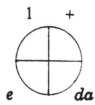

8. The "on beat" half of a pulse may be divided while the upbeat remains
    undivided or vice versa.

EXAMPLE

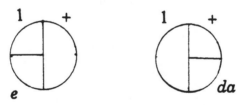

9. Note values that are divisible by two can also be divided by three—
    the divisions require a group bracket. The first portion is referred to by
    number, the other two portions are called *trip* and *let* respectively.

EXAMPLE

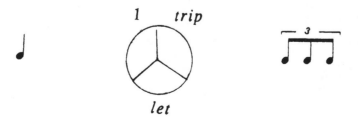

10. When dealing with a note value divisible by three, such as ♩., divisions by two require a group bracket.

EXAMPLE

11. Any pulse or subdivision can be divided and subdivided in a variety of ways. Some possible examples follow:

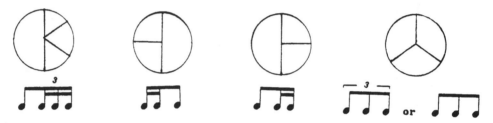

12. Subdivisions can be assigned sound or silence.

EXAMPLE
The darkened portions represent silence, or rests.

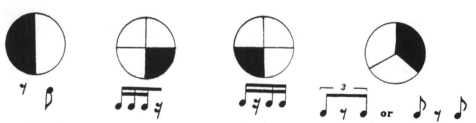

Group activities:
1. Select measures of rhythms from your band music. Assign students to diagram the rhythms and counting with circles.
2. Practice passages of music while tapping the foot to the beat. Watch carefully to ensure that students divide each beat evenly with the tapping, and that they do not tap out the written rhythms.

Name: _____

DURATION
Lesson Three—Assignment One

Part one: Write the appropriate rhythm represented by each circle according to the indicated pulse note.

1. $\frac{2}{2}$

2. $\frac{2}{4}$

3. $\frac{6}{8}$

4. $\frac{4}{4}$

5. $\frac{3}{4}$

DURATION, Lesson Three—Assignment One *(cont.)*

Part two: Above each of the following rhythms, represent each pulse by drawing an arrow down (↓) to indicate the beginning of the beat, and drawing an arrow up (↑) to represent the beginning of the upbeat.

EXAMPLE

1.

2.

3.

4.

5.

DURATION, Lesson Three—Assignment One *(cont.)*

Part three: Notate the rhythms represented by the counting names and appropriate for the given pulse note value.

1. $\frac{4}{4}$ 1 e + da

2. $\frac{2}{2}$ 1 e + da

3. $\frac{4}{4}$ 1 - + -

4. $\frac{4}{4}$ 1 - + da

5. $\frac{2}{2}$ 1 e + -

DURATION
Lesson Three—Assignment Two

Part one: Pay particular attention to the "incidental" sounds that surround you each day. (For example, a car blinker, factory machine, dishwasher, clothes dryer, child's toy, bird call, and so on.) Notate the rhythms of ten examples.

1. _____

2. _____

3. _____

4. _____

5. _____

6. _____

7. _____

8. _____

9. _____

10. _____

Part two: Organize the rhythmic elements of the ten examples into a composition.

_____

_____

_____

_____

_____

_____

_____

DURATION

Lesson Four

Lesson objective: To introduce the use of ties, dots, and syncopation.

Advance preparation: Examples of rhythms using ties and dots could be written on the board prior to lesson time.

Concept statements:

1. In musical notation, a *tie* is a curved line that connects two successive notes of the same pitch.

2. A tie is used to combine the duration value of the connected notes.

3. A tie is commonly used (1) to connect notes across a bar line, and (2) to create duration values that cannot be indicated by, or would be confusing written as a single note.

4. A *dot* placed after a note adds a duration value of one half that of the note itself.

5. A dot can be added to a note of any duration value. A dot has no value by itself, but is dependent upon the note that precedes it.

6. In some music, a double dot may be used. The second dot adds the duration value of half that of the first dot, or one-fourth that of the preceding note.

7. The purpose of a dot can always be achieved by using a tie, but the reverse is not true. *Consider the following examples and discuss why the use of a dot may seem awkward.*

8. Sometimes rhythms are arranged to form a stress pattern that seems to contradict the prevailing meter. Emphasis is displaced from a strong beat or part of a beat, to a weak beat or part of a beat. This is called *syncopation*.

9. Ties and dots are often used in notating syncopation.

EXAMPLE

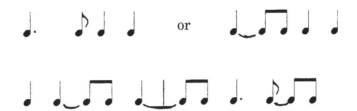

10. Syncopation is of two types: retardation (a sound suspended beyond the beat of the following pulse), and anticipation (sound placed earlier than expected and then suspended beyond the the beat of the following pulse).

EXAMPLE
retardation

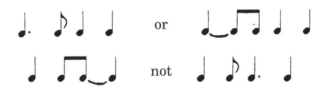

anticipation

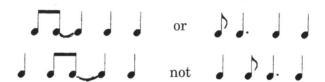

Group activities:

1. Invite students to write a syncopated rhythm on the board. Analyze each rhythm as a class to determine:

   a. if the rhythm is notated correctly,

   b. if the syncopation is anticipation or retardation type,

   c. if the rhythm could be written any other way (using dot, tie, alternate note grouping),

   d. how the rhythm could be applied to a scale or warm up etude.

   Play each rhythm as a class—on a single pitch or succession of pitches.

Name: _____

DURATION
Lesson Four—Assignment One

Part one: Use a tie or a dot, as indicated, to correctly rewrite each rhythm example.

1.

dot

6.

tie

2.

tie

7.

dot

3.

tie

8.

tie

4.

dot

9.

tie

5.

dot

10.

tie

DURATION, Lesson Four—Assignment One *(cont.)*

Part two: Identify each bracketed syncopation as follows: A = anticipation, or R = retardation.

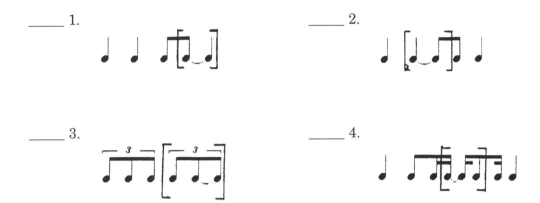

____ 1.

____ 2.

____ 3.

____ 4.

Part three: Play through the following excerpts on your instrument. Then rewrite the rhythms with at least two examples of syncopation in each.

1.

Moderately   Mason

2.

Andante   *Welsh Air*

DURATION

Lesson Five

Lesson objectives: (1) To describe simple, compound and complex meters. (2) To introduce the terms triplet and duplet as ways of notating irregular subdivisions.

Advance preparation: Write the rhythm examples on the chalkboard, and have a metronome for demonstration.

Concept statements:

1. *Simple meters* use pulse note values that are divisible by two. The pulse notes of simple meters are typically the quarter or half note. Written as 2/4, 2/2, C, 3/4, 2/ ♩, and so on.

2. Pulse notes in simple meters can be divided by three, but are notated using a figure known as the *triplet*.

EXAMPLE

3. *Compound meters* use pulse note values divisible by three. Typical pulse notes of compound meters are the dotted eighth ♪·, the dotted quarter ♩·, and the dotted half ♩·:

EXAMPLE

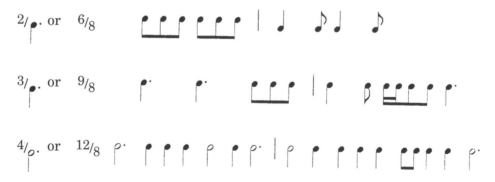

4. Pulse notes in compound meters can be divided into two, but are notated using a figure called a *duplet*.

EXAMPLE

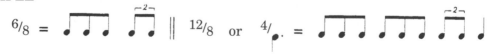

5. In compound and simple meters, each pulse is considered equidistant from other pulses. In *complex meters*, pulses within a measure may expand or contract as determined by the grouping of subdivisions. As in compound meters, the meter signature of complex meters indicates the number and type of *subdivisions* per measure. Typical rhythms and complex meters follow:

EXAMPLE

2 pulses
5 divisions   written $\frac{5}{8}$

2 pulses
5 divisions   written $\frac{5}{4}$

3 pulses
7 divisions   written $\frac{7}{8}$

4 pulses
12 divisions   written $\frac{12}{8}$

Group activities:

1. Select music from your band folder and identify passages as simple, compound, or complex meters.

2. Select a short passage from your band folder and rewrite the simple meter as compound and vice versa. Rewrite the rhythms in the new meter replacing regular subdivisions with duplets or triplets and vice versa.

Name: _____

DURATION
Lesson Five—Assignment One

Part one: Write an appropriate meter signature and identify the meter as follows:
S = simple, C = compound, and X = complex.

DURATION, Lesson Five—Assignment One *(cont.)*

Part two: In each measure, fill in the blank with a duplet or triplet to make an irregular subdivision.

1. $\frac{2}{4}$ ♩ ___

2. $\frac{6}{8}$ ___ ♩ ♪

3. $\frac{12}{8}$ ♩ ♪ ___ ♫♩ ♪

4. $\frac{3}{4}$ ___

Part three: Write the appropriate pulse notes above each division group. Identify each meter as S = simple, C = compound, or X = complex.

EXAMPLE

S $\frac{4}{4}$ X $\frac{7}{8}$ C $\frac{6}{8}$

___ 1. $\frac{12}{8}$ ___ 2. $\frac{7}{8}$

___ 3. $\frac{4}{4}$ ___ 4. $\frac{5}{8}$

___ 5. $\frac{11}{16}$ ___ 6. $\frac{3}{4}$

___ 7. $\frac{7}{8}$ ___ 8. $\frac{3}{8}$

___ 9. $\frac{5}{8}$ ___ 10. $\frac{3}{16}$

DURATION

Lesson Six

Lesson objective: To introduce the concept of changing meters and the notation used to establish pulse from one meter to another.

Advance preparation: Have a metronome for demonstration.

Concept statements:

1. Within any composition, the stress pattern can shift from groups of three to groups of four and vice versa. A shift in stress pattern is called *changing meter.*

2. When changing meters, it is essential that the written music also include a marking to establish the tempo and pulse relationship of the two meters.

3. Typically, there are two types of meter changes: (1) changes in which the pulse note value and its divisions remain constant from one meter to another, and (2) changes in pulse note value in one of four ways:

   pulse to pulse

   $$\frac{2}{4} \text{ to } \frac{6}{8} \text{ or } \frac{4}{4} \text{ to } \frac{2}{2}$$

   division to division

   $$\frac{4}{4} \text{ to } \frac{6}{8}$$

   division to pulse

   $$\frac{7}{8} \text{ to } \frac{3}{4}$$

   pulse to division

   $$\frac{4}{8} \text{ to } \frac{2}{\dot{2}}.$$

100

Group activities:

1. Practice the following meter changes with the various pulse and tempo indications.

DURATION
Lesson Six—Assignment One

Part one: Circle the bar line that marks a meter change.

1.

2.

3.

4.

Part two: Identify each meter change according to the following code:

1 = first and most simple type meter change (pulse note value and its divisions remain constant);

2 = change in pulse note value;
    a = pulse to pulse
    b = division to division
    c = division to pulse
    d = pulse to division

Name: _____

DURATION
Unit Quiz

Part one: Write the counting above each rhythm, indicate beat and upbeat with a down and up arrow.

1. (rhythm in 2/8)   5. (rhythm in 3/4)

2. (rhythm in 4/4)   6. (rhythm in 3/2)

3. (rhythm in 4/8)   7. (rhythm in 2/2)

4. (rhythm in 3/4)   8. (rhythm in 5/4)

©1998 by Parker Publishing Company, Inc.

103

DURATION Unit Quiz (cont.)

Part two: Identify meters as S = simple, C = compound, X = complex, and write pulse notes above division groupings.

Part three: Use mathematic symbols < (less than), > (greater than), = (equal to), to show the relationship of each figure's total duration value. Consider the pairs in the same meter.

EXAMPLE

DURATION Unit Quiz *(cont.)*

Part four: Circle the syncopated rhythms in the following examples.

Part five: Write an appropriate marking for the types of meter changes indicated.

1. Pulse to pulse
   [   ]
   2/4 to 2/2

2. Division to division
   [   ]
   4/4 to 12/8

3. No change in pulse note value
   [   ]
   3/4 to 4/4

4. Pulse to division
   [   ]
   4/8 to 4/4

5. Division to pulse
   [   ]
   7/8 to 3/4

Unit Four

ACOUSTICS

Acoustics Vocabulary List

Acoustics Vocabulary Worksheet

Lesson One

To discuss the characteristics of pitch, timbre and loudness and the acoustic principles that govern them.

Lesson Two

To present the various groups of instruments and the basic characteristics of each group.

Lesson Three

To describe the harmonic series and its general relationship to wind instruments.

Lesson Four

To explain the relationship of various characteristics of acoustic phenomena to wind instruments, i.e., conical and cylindrical bores, whole and half tubes, transposing and non-transposing, keys, valves, slides and crooks.

Lesson Five

To explain the terms tone quality and intonation and suggest ways of applying acoustic principles to improve both.

Acoustics Unit Quiz

ACOUSTICS
Vocabulary List

Acoustics   The study of the qualities and characteristics of sound.

Amplitude   The measurement of sound intensity.

Beats   In tuning, the phasing in and out of two unequal pitch frequencies.

Brass   The family of instruments made of brass or other metal.

Cent   A unit of measurement for frequencies (one hundredth of a semitone) as determined by the equally tempered scale.

Conical   The shape of an instrument's bore, or diameter, that tapers at one end.

Crook   An attachment for brass instruments that alters the length of the instrument tube.

Cup   The shape of brass instrument mouthpieces, except the French horn.

Cylindrical   The shape of an instrument's bore, or diameter, that stays constant — does not taper.

Dynamics   A term for music loudness and softness.

Embouchure   The proper position of the lips in the playing of wind instruments.

Equally-Tempered Scale   The chromatic scale resultant from dividing an octave into twelve equal semitones instead of the exact frequencies produced naturally in the harmonic series.

Frequency   The number of complete sound waves occurring per unit of time. Commonly measured in cycles per second.

Fundamental   The lowest harmonic in a harmonic series. The generating tone of partials, or overtones.

Funnel   The shape of a French horn mouthpiece.

Half-Tube   Instruments for which the slightest air pressure will set up vibrations of half the length of the instrument's tube, thus making the fundamental, or pedal tone, nearly impossible to produce.

Harmonic Intonation   Tuning to a sounded reference pitch or pitches—either unison or interval combinations.

Harmonic Series   The pattern of pitches produced by a fundamental and its overtones.

108

©1998 by Parker Publishing Company, Inc.

Humoring	Altering raising or lowering pitch while sustaining a tone.
Intensity	The energy imparted to a string or air column determining the resultant sound's loudness.
Key Mechanism	The system of covering and opening the tone, or side holes of woodwind instruments.
Melodic Intonation	Tuning of intervals in a melody according to memory of preceding pitches.
Mouthpiece	The part of a wind instrument that is inserted into the mouth, or applied to the lips.
Overtone	Pitches above the fundamental that are produced by vibrations in segments of the entire string or air column length.
Partial	Another name for overtone.
Percussion	A family of instruments who's sound is produced by striking one object with another.
Pitch Intensity	The focus on precise placement of pitch.
Reed	A thin piece of cane or other material that is fixed in place but allowed to vibrate freely at one end. Single reeds vibrate against the slot of the mouthpiece to which they are attached. Double reeds are attached to and vibrate against each other.
Slide	A length of tube that slips over another tube and thus can adjust the overall length of an instrument.
Tendencies	The intonation inclinations of certain pitches.
Timbre	The quality of sound that makes it distinct from other sounds.
Tone Quality	Another name for timbre.
Transposing	Instruments built in keys that necessitate written notes different than sounding pitches.
Tuning	The process of pitch adjustment.
Valves	Mechanisms that divert the air column through different tube lengths on brass instruments.
Volume	Loudness or softness of music.
Whole Tube	Instruments that easily vibrate the entire length of air column and thus produce the pedal tone, or fundamental.
Woodwinds	The family of instruments in which sound is produced by the vibration of reeds or splitting air across a wedge.

Name: _____

ACOUSTICS
Vocabulary Worksheet

Part one: Identify each statement with a "T" for true and an "F" for false.

____ 1. The *woodwind* family includes only instruments that use a reed.

____ 2. An increase in *amplitude* also means a change in pitch.

____ 3. *Funnel* refers to an instrument's bore, or diameter.

____ 4. A note played soft, then loud, is a change in *dynamics*.

____ 5. *Frequency* is the measurement of sound wave cycles per second.

____ 6. Matching the frequencies of two unison pitches is an example of *tuning*.

____ 7. The *harmonic series* includes a fundamental and its *overtones*.

____ 8. A *half-tube* instrument does not sound its fundamental easily.

____ 9. The *equally tempered scale* is comprised of twelve equal semitones within an octave.

____10. *Timbre* is the quality that distinguishes the sound of an oboe from the sound of a trumpet.

Part two: Complete each sentence with the vocabulary word most appropriate.

1. When tuning one pitch against another, _____ are the sounds that indicate unequal frequencies.

2. The study of qualities and characteristics of sound is called _____.

3. Instruments that sound a pitch different than their written note are called _____.

4. Tuning a pitch of a melody by memory of previous pitches and the correct intervals is called _____ intonation.

5. A trombone _____ slips over another piece of tubing and can adjust the length of the air column.

Part three: Select the answer that best represents the relationship described.

1. Embouchure to playing an instrument is like:
   a. water is to plants
   b. racquet grip is to tennis
   c. color/tint is to paint

2. Humoring to pitch is like:
   a. tightening is to a screw
   b. air conditioning is to heat
   c. fine tuning is to a radio station

3. A reed to a clarinet is like:
   a. a valve is to a tuba
   b. lips are to a trumpet
   c. a stick is to a drum

4. Overtone to partial is like:
   a. timbre is to intensity
   b. pedal tone is to fundamental
   c. brass is to woodwind

©1998 by Parker Publishing Company, Inc.

ACOUSTICS

Lesson One

Lesson objective: To discuss the characteristics of pitch, timbre, and loudness and the acoustic principles that govern them.

Advance preparation: To help the students visualize the described events with sound vibration, have a suspended string for demonstration (a guitar, violin, or bass will do). Also, a simple, open tube such as a segment of garden hose or pipe.

Concept statements:

1. All sound is produced and perceived by vibration.

2. Musical instruments shape sound vibrations and transmit them through the air to a listening ear.

3. Various characteristics of sound vibration determine our perceptions of *pitch*, *loudness*, and *timbre*.

4. In discussing characteristics of vibration, it is helpful to visualize a string stretched from point X to Y. On a wind instrument, a column of air is comparable to the string.

5. A plucked string vibrates back and forth across its original position. The number of complete vibrations per second is called *frequency*.

6. Generally, differences in frequency determine differences in pitch.

7. Alterations in the frequency of vibration can be made by (1) adjusting the length of string or the air column, or (2) adjusting the tension of the string or the speed of the air through the tube.

8. Tightening a drum head, reducing instrument length (either by uncovering a tone hole or shortening the tube), or increasing the speed of the air will raise the pitch of an instrument (except on clarinet or saxophone). Adjustments to the reverse will cause a lower pitch.

9. Generally, the height of a vibration is measured as *amplitude* and determines the *intensity*, or loudness, of sound.

10. The intensity of a sound is influenced by the amount of energy transmitted to the sounding device.

11. The pitch of a string or air column vibrating in its entire length is called the *fundamental*.

12. Strings and air columns vibrate in their entire length and segments thereof simultaneously. The segment vibrations produce pitches less perceivable than the fundamental. These pitches are called *overtones*, or *partials*.

13. The presence or absence of perceivable overtones and their intensity is the main influence in our perception of *timbre*, or tone color.

14. The physical structure of an instrument largely determines the intensity of overtones and therefore its timbre. However, the musician is responsible for playing correctly and producing the *characteristic sound* of the instrument.

15. The principle of overtones explains the production of various notes from any one fingering (or length of tubing).

Group activities:

1. Analyze each band instrument according to:

   a. method of sound production—vibrating lips, reed, membrane, or splitting air.

   b. method of changing tube length—tone holes, slides, crooks, etc.

   c. the range of volume possible.

   d. the change in timbre and how it can be manipulated.

2. Check into the possibility of viewing a video or filmstrip that treats the subject of acoustics.

3. Extend a string between two points and experiment with the various characteristics of vibration.

Name: _____

ACOUSTICS
Lesson One—Assignment One

Part one: Beneath each diagram, list the words most related to the concept shown.

volume   amplitude   overtone   frequency
pitch   timbre   intensity   harmonics

A.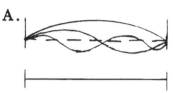

B. VIBRATIONS IN TIME

C. 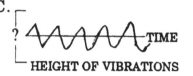 TIME / HEIGHT OF VIBRATIONS

Part two: Next to each statement, indicate the *most apparent* change that will occur in the sound of the instrument when played. Use the following letters: H=higher pitch; L=lower pitch; F=louder; P=softer; T=changed timbre.

____ 1. Tightening a guitar string.

____ 2. Striking a drum harder.

____ 3. Loosening a timpani head.

____ 4. "Biting" the reed.

____ 5. Opening another tone hole.

____ 6. Extending a trombone slide.

____ 7. Improving posture and air support.

____ 8. Pressing the brass instrument mouthpiece more tightly against the lips.

____ 9. Playing just the head joint of a flute.

____10. Combining two people on a unison note.

ACOUSTICS

Lesson Two

Lesson objective: To present the various groups of instruments and the basic characteristics of each group.

Advance preparation: Have pictures or actual examples of many instruments, reeds, mouthpieces, bows, and so on. Someone available to demonstrate basic playing technique and sound production of each instrument type. A recording of Benjamin Britten's "Young Person's Guide to the Orchestra" for use in identifying the sounds of basic orchestra instruments.

Concept statements:

1. Western instruments are commonly grouped into four categories; *strings*, *percussion*, *winds*, and *electronic*.

2. Instrument categories are determined by the means of sound production.

3. *String* instruments are those with strings to be plucked, strummed, bowed, or struck.

4. Members of the string instrument group include guitars, violins, cellos, piano, harpsichord, lute, and many others.

5. *Wind* instruments are those that generate sound by setting a column of air into motion.

6. The main wind instruments are divided into two groups:
   brass—including trombone, tuba, trumpet, horn, and baritone.
   woodwinds—including clarinet, oboe, saxophone, bassoon, and flute.

7. Brass instruments are so named because of the brass or other metal used in their construction. In this instrument group, vibrations are initiated by air passing through the players' lips and then are transmitted to a tube by way of a cup- or funnel-shaped mouthpiece.

8. Woodwind instruments are those in which vibration is initiated by air activating a reed or pair or reeds. Flutes produce sound by splitting the air stream across the embouchure hole. Regardless of the fact that flutes do not use a reed, they are still considered part of the *woodwind* family.

9. Percussion instruments traditionally have been defined as those sounded by shaking, or striking.

114

10. Percussion instruments are numerous and varied but of those common-ly used, two groups can be identfied:
    Pitched percussion—those from which a specific pitch is intended such as timpani, xylophone, bells, marimba, chimes and celesta.
    Non-pitched percussion—those instruments which may be once *tuned*, but not intended to imply a specific pitch such as snare drum, triangle, cymbals, bass drum and woodblock.

11. *Electronic instruments* are those which produce acoustical vibrations with electronic means.

Group activities:

1. Examine instrument types and experiment with sound production and manipulation.

2. Invite class members or special guests to perform compositions that demonstrate the capabilities of their instruments.

3. Assign class members to invent, construct and demonstrate instruments according to the principles of sound production discussed.

4. Organize small ensembles of non-traditional instrumentations in order to experiment with various timbre combinations.

Name: _____

ACOUSTICS
Lesson Two—Assignment One

Part one: Group the following instruments under their most definitive category headings: Snare drum, tenor saxophone, cello, trumpet, baritone, bassoon, suspended cymbal, flute, oboe, chimes, piano, harpsichord, trombone, tuba, timpani, tambourine, soprano saxophone, alto flute, viola, English horn, French horn.

BRASS   **WOODWINDS**   **STRINGS**

PITCHED PERCUSSION   **NON-PITCHED PERCUSSION**

ACOUSTICS, Lesson Two—Assignment One *(cont.)*

Part two: For each instrument listed, name at least two characteristic elements of its sound production.

EXAMPLE
Cymbals—vibrations caused by striking one against another. The sound is not intended to imply definite pitch.

OBOE

TRUMPET

BASSOON

SAXOPHONE

TIMPANI

GUITAR

TUBA

CELLO

Part three: Select ten different instruments of your choice and assign a symbol to represent a general sound (non-specific pitch or volume) from each. Write a legend describing what the symbols represent and then compose an eight-measure piece utilizing the sounds of your selected instruments.

EXAMPLE

LEGEND

$ = trumpet	* = triangle	~ = tuba	# = tambourine	< = oboe
@ = piano	% = saxophone	M = cello	& = clarinet	: = snare

ACOUSTICS

Lesson Three

Lesson objective: To describe the harmonic series and its general relationship to wind instruments.

Advance preparation: Staff lines on the chalkboard or large chart, and staff paper for students. Also, a suspended string and open tube (a short piece of hose or pipe) to help illustrate the acoustic principles discussed.

Concept statements:

1. An enclosed column of air, or a suspended string vibrating in its entire wave length produces a frequency and pitch called the *fundamental*.

2. The longer the tube enclosing the air column, or the longer the string, the lower the fundamental pitch.

3. Vibrating systems generally vibrate at several wave lengths simultaneously. For example, a string vibrates in its total length as well as in halves, thirds, fourths, and so on.

4. As the string vibrates in half its total length, it produces a frequency twice that of the fundamental, the segment of thirds produces a frequency three times that of the fundamental, and so on.

5. The vibrating segments of the fundamental sound wave are called *overtones*, or *partials*—frequencies and pitches *higher* than the fundamental.

6. The series of frequencies consisting of the fundamental and its overtones is called the *harmonic series*. Any individual pitch of the harmonic series can be called a *harmonic*. The fundamental pitch is called the first harmonic, the next is the second, and so on.

7. The harmonic series of any fundamental wave length follows a pattern of successive intervals. (See the pattern or *harmonic series* on the following page).

8. The harmonic series is a very important influence in the construction of instruments and their fingering systems.

119

THE HARMONIC SERIES

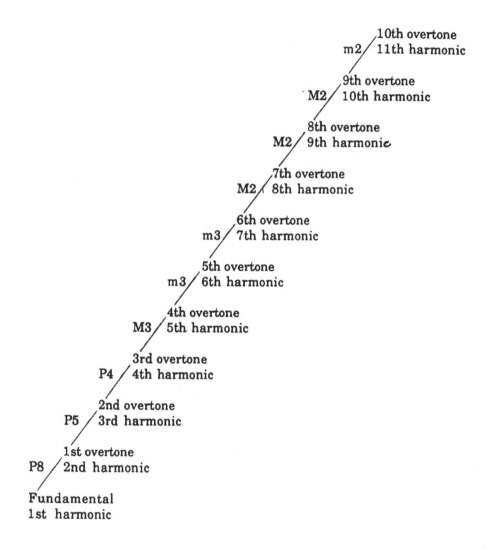

10th overtone
m2 / 11th harmonic

9th overtone
M2 / 10th harmonic

8th overtone
M2 / 9th harmonic

7th overtone
M2 / 8th harmonic

6th overtone
m3 / 7th harmonic

5th overtone
m3 / 6th harmonic

4th overtone
M3 / 5th harmonic

3rd overtone
P4 / 4th harmonic

2nd overtone
P5 / 3rd harmonic

1st overtone
P8 / 2nd harmonic

Fundamental
1st harmonic

Group activities:

1. Determine the lowest fundamental pitch possible in your band class. Have the player of that instrument play the fundamental and then every possible note of the harmonic series. Try to name the expected pitches before they are played.

2. Practice singing the intervals of the harmonic series in their proper sequence.

Name: _____

ACOUSTICS
Lesson Three—Assignment One

Part one: For each of the fundamental pitches given, write the pitches of the harmonic series to the seventh partial or overtone.

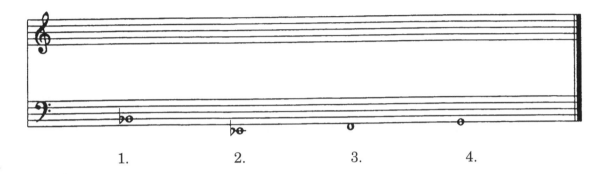

1.   2.   3.   4.

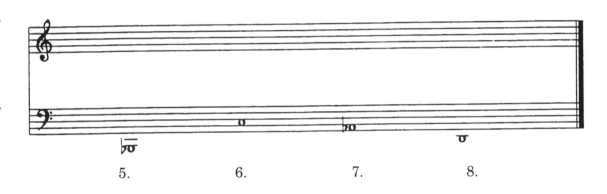

5.   6.   7.   8.

ACOUSTICS

Lesson Four

Lesson objective: To explain the relationship of various characteristics of acoustic phenomena to wind instruments; i.e., conical and cylindrical bores, whole and half tubes, transposing and non-transposing, keys, valves, slides and crooks.

Advance preparation: Have wind instruments available to demonstrate the principles discussed.

Concept statements:

1. Each type of wind instrument is unique in the way it is designed to respond to the principles of acoustics, but divisions can be made according to some general characteristics.

2. Wind instruments are categorized into acoustical groups of either *conical bore*—expanding diameter (cone shape), or *cylindrical bore*—constant diameter. (Bore shape is determined without consideration of the instrument bell.)

3. The bore of the instrument is a major factor in determining the character of the sound produced.

4. Conical bore instruments include: tuba, cornet, French horn, baritone, oboe, saxophone and bassoon.

5. Cylindrical bore instruments include: trumpet, trombone, flute, and clarinet.

6. A pipe or tube of given length produces the fundamental pitch. However by *overblowing*, which requires proper control of the breath and lips, one of the overtones can be made to sound.

7. All the overtones possible from any given tube length are called the instrument's *natural tones*.

8. Another name for an instrument's fundamental is *pedal tone*.

9. In a number of instruments, the pedal tone is almost impossible to produce. In explaining this charateristic, a distinction is made between *whole-tube* instruments, in which the air column will vibrate as a whole and thus produce the pedal tone, and *half-tube* instruments, in which the slightest air pressure will cause the vibrations at half the length and thus produce the the first overtone.

10. Whole-tube instruments include all the woodwinds and the large bore brasses—tubas. (Some exceptionally skilled players have been able to obtain the pedal tone on the small bore brasses.)

11. Tubes and pipes can be described as *open pipes* or *closed pipes* as determined by an open end or stopped end. All common wind instuments are actually open pipes. The clarinet, however, has unique qualities that combine with the cylindrical bore to cause it to react like a closed pipe.

12. Overblowing the clarinet produces a pitch one twelfth higher than the fundamental, and only the odd numbered overtones can be produced. All other wind instruments overblow the octave and can produce all overtones.

13. The fundamental pitch of an instrument determines its key name: "B♭ trumpet," "E♭ saxophone," "C flute," and so on.

14. For some instruments, the written notes are given different names than their actual sounding notes. These are called *transposing instruments* and include saxophones, clarinets, trumpets, French horns, cornets and baritones (when the part is written for treble clef).

15. For any tube or instrument length there are gaps between the pitches of the harmonic series (the instrument's natural tones). In order to bridge this gap and obtain all the semitones between partials, various means have been devised to temporarily shorten or lengthen the instrument.

16. There are four main types of devices used to alter instrument length:
    a. *Slides*—commonly used on *slide* trombones. Two separate portions of tubing, one sliding inside an outer sleeve to offer lengths of the original tube; the length of the original tube plus partial extensions of the outer sleeve; or the full inner tube and sleeve lengths combined.
    b. *Crooks* or shanks—not commonly used today, but a popular method of length adjustment in trumpets and horns during the 18th century. Loops of various length tubing were exchanged in the trumpet as needed for compositions or sections in specific keys.
    c. *Valves*—commonly found on brass insrtuments such as trumpets, horns, tubas, and so on. Actually the system consists of several crooks permanently attached to the instrument, to be opened and closed momentarily by the means of valves. By opening a valve, the crook's length is added to that of the natural tube. Normally the instrument is provided with three valves (I, II, III), that lower the pitch by 2, 1, or 3 semitones respectively. Combinations of valves lower the pitch by 4, 5, or 6 semitones.
    d. *Side holes*—commonly found only in woodwind instruments. Side holes are holes bored into the side walls of the instrument that can be opened or closed with the fingers and key mechanisms. If all the holes are closed or covered, the pipe sounds its fundamental. Uncovered holes shorten the air column and produce higher pitches.

Group activities:

1. Select a unison passage of music and assign all players instruments of conical bore to play it for the rest of the class. Repeat the same passage played only by players of instruments of cylindrical bore. Discuss any noticeable differences in timbre.

2. Invite students who play transposing instruments to explain how they must respond to the director's instructions in "concert pitch."

3. To experience and practice the principles of overblowing to produce overtones, at least in the brass sections, try the following warm-up exercise:

(All written notes are concert pitch)

Woodwinds

Brass (All notes should be played with "open horns" except in the F Horns which must "finger" certain notes.)

After playing the exercise on open horns, repeat the sequence one half-step lower (II valve), one whole-step lower (I valve), and so on.

©1998 by Parker Publishing Company, Inc.

Name: _____

ACOUSTICS
Lesson Four—Assignment One

Part one: Examine the brass instruments named and use mathematic equivalence symbols (>, <, =) to show the greatest value as the fingering that will produce *the lowest fundamental pitch.*

Trumpet: F Horn: Tuba:

II   ___ I   III ___ I   I+III   ___ II

III   ___ I+II   I   ___ III+II   I+II+III   ___ III

I+III ___ I+II   II   ___ III   Open   ___ I

Part two: Identify the transposing instruments by placing a "T" in the blank next to the instrument's name. Identify the non-transposing instruments with an "N."

____ Saxophone   ____ Tuba   ____ Oboe   ____ Flute   ____ Bassoon

____ Trombone   ____ Clarinet   ____ Trumpet   ____ F Horn

Part three: Select three transposing instruments from the previous assignment section and write the pitch they would *read* in order to produce a concert C.

Instrument   **Written pitch . . . . . . to sound;**   **or;**

1. _____

2. _____

3. _____

ACOUSTICS, Lesson Four—Assignment One *(cont.)*

Part four: Beneath each instrument listed, identify all applicable characteristics according to the following code:

Co. = conical bore
Cy. = cylindrical bore

PT = attainable pedal tone
NPT = pedal tone not attainable

V = valve
SH = side hole
S = slide

O = open tube
C = closed tube (or responds like one)

T = transposing
NT = non-transposing

TUBA

TRUMPET

FLUTE

CLARINET

F HORN

SAXOPHONE

BASSOON

TROMBONE

ACOUSTICS

Lesson Five

Lesson objective: To explain the terms tone quality and intonation and suggest ways of applying acoustic principles to improve both.

Advance preparation: Have various instruments available for demonstration and an electronic device for producing a reference pitch and calculating the "in tuneness" of pitch.

Concept statements:

1. The principles of acoustics directly affect the sound produced by every player and his instrument.

2. The first goal of a player should be to produce the timbre or quality of tone that is characteristic of his instrument.

3. Generally, the most characteristic timbre, or tone quality, of a wind instrument is the tone produced with:

    a. the most efficient supply of breath.
    b. the most efficient embouchure set.
    c. the appropriate intensity, or loudness for the musical setting.
    d. the appropriate style for the musical setting.
    e. the proper placement of pitch intensity.

4. Even when the conditions described above are met, the quality of tone can further be influenced by the condition of the instrument itself, or its mouthpiece or reed.

5. Impediments to the air flow throughout the instrument, or air leakage from a partially covered tone hole affect the overall tone quality.

6. Splits and chips in a reed, or dents in a mouthpiece shank have detrimental effects on sound wave vibration and therefore the timbre of sound. In order to produce a correct quality of tone, the instrument and all its parts must be in good working condition.

7. Concurrent with quality tone production, an important challenge for wind players is achieving correct pitch placement or *intonation*.

8. *Melodic intonation* is the ability to play exact intervals from note to note of a melody. The aural memory is one means for comparing a previous pitch to each new pitch produced, however, an electronic tuning device, which measures the frequencies of a pitch played into it and shows the degrees—measured in "*cents*," of out-of-tuneness can also be used. In either case, melodic intonation requires concentration and much practice.

127

9. *Harmonic intonation* is the ability to match pitches as unisons or play the correct intervals of harmony. Harmonic intonation requires the player to compare existing tones and work to place his own pitch precisely among the others.

10. Correct tuning of unisons will result in two vibratory frequencies that are equal. Correct tuning of intervals will generally produce two frequencies that are of correct ratios for octaves and other intervals.

11. A musician does not consider the literal characteristics of vibratory frequency as he performs. He can determine if his tones are in the correct frequency ratio by the presence or absence of *tuning beats*. This principle is best understood by describing the tuning of a unison.

12. According to the definition of pitch, two instruments sounding the same pitch will be vibrating sound waves at exactly the same frequencies. This condition would produce sound *absent* of tuning beats. If two instruments sound pitches with frequencies differing by one vibration per second, a short, but audibly louder sound will occur once per second. These louder sounds are known as tuning beats. The number of beats per second is determined by the difference in frequency of the two pitches. The greater the "out of tuneness," the faster the beats.

13. When tuning beats are present, one of the players must adjust his pitch, higher or lower, until the beats slow down and eventually stop.

14. Tuning consonant intervals can be done in the same way as unisons, however, the beats are sometimes harder to recognize. Because consonant pitches have related frequencies (one is an even ratio of the other), the wave lengths vibrate syncronously unless one is out of tune.

15. There are numerous influences on the tuning of instruments, individual pitches and ensembles.

    a. *Temperature*—changes in temperature initiate changes in density of air and substance. Sound waves are impeded in thick air (cold temperature increases density, warm air decreases density) and most instruments will accordingly rise in pitch as the temperature rises.

    b. *Intonation deficiencies of instruments*—in instrument manufacturing, some compromises in pitch must be made to accommodate the *equally tempered scale* (the division of an octave into twelve equal semitones). On every wind instrument there are some pitches that are especially difficult to play in tune.

    c. *Harmonic intonation tendencies*—several pitches of the harmonic series will be slightly out of tune because of the equally tempered scale. Generally the tendencies of the *harmonics* are as follows:

8th	in tune
7th	extremely flat
6th	very sharp
5th	slightly flat
4th	in tune
3rd	slightly sharp
2nd	in tune
1st	(fundamental)

   d. *Length or width of the instrument tube*—instruments are designed to play most pitches in tune when the instrument tube is at its intended length and width, and when the instrument is free from dents or dirt in the bore or tone holes.

16. Intonation of individual instruments and an ensemble can be improved by applying the following techniques:

   a. *Initial warm up and tuning*—the temperature of the instrument itself, and the air column inside it can be somewhat stabilized by blowing warm air through the instrument tube, either as a determined pitch or simply an air stream. After warm up, a reference tone can be electronically produced and individuals can work to match the reference pitch by tuning out the beats. During the subsequent rehearsal, continuous attention must be paid to the ensemble pitch and each member's need to match.

   b. *Humoring*—this refers to the ability of players to raise or lower pitch while holding a tone. Humoring can be effected by

      (1) tightening the lips to raise the pitch, and vice versa,
      (2) increasing air pressure to raise the pitch (except on the clarinet and saxophone which go flat when the tone is *forced*),
      (3) using vibrato,
      (4) altering the shape of the oral cavity—arching the tongue to raise a pitch and leveling the tongue to lower a pitch, or opening and closing the back of the throat,
      (5) various changes in pressure on the reed, hand in the bell, direction of air stream, and so on, as are applicable to specific instruments.

   c. *Alternate fingerings*—because of their place in numerous harmonic series, some pitches can be obtained by using various fingerings. Each instrumentalist should become familiar with the alternate fingerings unique to his instrument.

   d. *Compensating mechanisms*—especially in the brass, attachments have been devised to alter the pitch of tones most difficult to tune. These mechanisms include extra valves, and levers to extend first and third valve slides.

Group activities:

1. Practice tuning out beats in unisons and intervals with different instrument combinations.

2. Demonstrate timbre and pitch tendencies of various qualities of instruments, mouthpieces, reeds, fingerings and so on.

3. Practice *humoring* a pitch by sustaining a unison and at the director's signal of hands vertically apart, each wind player *bend* the pitch to the degree of the spread of the hands. As the hands come together, each wind player brings the pitch back into focus. The director should raise the top hand from the bottom to indicate bending the pitch up, and lower the bottom hand from the top to indicate bending the pitch down.

Name: _____

ACOUSTICS
Lesson Five—Assignment One

Part one: Name and describe two ways of humoring pitch on your instrument.

1. _____

2. _____

Part two: Name and describe three adverse effects on instrument pitch, and/or tone quality.

1. _____

2. _____

3. _____

Part three: List three pitches that are characteristically out of tune on *your* instrument. Describe an alternate fingering if available. (Consult with a private instructor, or use an electronic tuner).

1. _____

2. _____

3. _____

Name: _____

ACOUSTICS
Unit Quiz

Part one: Next to each statement, mark the letter of the diagram that best illustrates the principle described.

A.

B.

C.

D.

_____ 1. Gradual increase in volume.

_____ 2. Presence or absence determines timbre.

_____ 3. Unison pitches out of tune.

_____ 4. Playing with more energy and intensity.

_____ 5. A short melody.

_____ 6. Frequency "beats."

_____ 7. Pitches obtainable by "overblowing."

_____ 8. Vibrating whole and segments.

_____ 9. Change in amplitude.

_____ 10. Intonation problem.

ACOUSTICS, Unit Quiz *(cont.)*

Part two: Fill in the blank with the word that correctly completes the sentence.

1. An electronic tuning device indicates out of tuneness in terms of _____ sharp or flat.

2. Instrument tubes are of cylindrical or _____ bore.

3. One method of humoring involves moving the _____ to change the shape of the oral cavity.

4. The harmonic series includes a fundamental and the partials or _____ above the fundamental.

5. Different types of instruments (bassoons from trumpets, from clarinets and so on), tend to sound overtones in varying degrees of intensity and thereby have differing _____.

6. Instruments that sound different tones than those written for them are called _____ instruments.

7. *Pedal tone* is another word for an instrument's _____ pitch.

8. Two "consonant" pitches of varying frequencies will produce _____.

9. Using a trumpet third valve instead of the first/second combination is an example of _____ fingering.

10. As temperature rises, most instruments will _____ in pitch.

Part three: Write in the missing partials of the harmonic series and identify the pitch tendencies of three different partials.

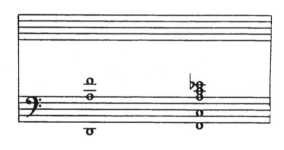

      1.   2.   3.   4.

Unit Five

STYLE

Style Vocabulary List

Style Vocabulary Worksheet

Lesson One
> To outline music style periods and discuss Greek influence on the development of music.

Lesson Two
> To present information regarding the style of music in the Medieval Period.

Lesson Three
> To present information regarding the style of music of the Renaissance Period.

Lesson Four
> To present information regarding the music of the Baroque Period.

Lesson Five
> To present information regarding music of the Classical Period.

Lesson Six
> To present information regarding music of the Romantic Period.

Lesson Seven
> To present information regarding art music of the Twentieth Century Period.

Style Unit Quiz

STYLE
Vocabulary List

Alberti Bass   Accompaniment consisting of repeated broken chords.

Aleatory   Music in which one or more elements are left to the descretion of the performers which results in unpredictability or chance.

Antiphony   Lines of music alternated between one "choir" and another.

Ars Antiqua   A term used to describe music of the 12th and 13th centuries ("old art").

Ars Nova   A term used to describe music of the 14th century ("new art").

Baroque   A musical style period from 1600–1750. Characterized by the use of basso continuo, and extreme contrasts to represent "states of the soul."

Chamber Music   Instrumental ensemble music performed by one player for each part.

Chant   General term used to describe monophonic music of the medieval style era characterized by narrow range, and unmeasured rhythm and meter.

Chromaticism   The use of some tones of the chromatic scale in addition to those of the diatonic scale. An important musical characteristic of 16th century madrigals and music of the late 19th and early 20th centuries.

Classical   Music style period from 1750–1825. Characterized by distinct phrases of two or four measures, and the use of Alberti bass.

Ethos   The ancient Greek philosophy that music influenced "character" of listeners.

Folk Music   Music which originates from the common people of a culture.

Hocket   The division of a melodic line into fragments to be sung by seperate voices.

Jazz   A style of music developed in the United States during the 20th century. Characterized by the use of improvised melodies.

Leitmotif   A short melody or theme consistently associated with particular characters, objects, or ideas.

Libretto   The book of text of an opera or oratorio.

Lyrical   A smooth, singing quality.

Medieval	A musical style period generally associated with music prior to 1450. Characterized by music including chant, organum, and motet.
Melismatic	A term used to describe the singing of many tones to a single syllable of text in chant.
Motet	A polyphonic, vocal composition usually sung without accompaniment that originated in the medieval era.
Musique Concrete	A musical style developed in the 20th century. Characterized by the use of tape recordings of sounds and noises and the avoidance of traditional instruments.
Neo-Classical	The 20th century renewed interest in the compositional forms of the classical style period.
Oratorio	A composition for solo voices, choir, and orchestra.
Polyphony	Music texture of two or more melodic lines sounding simultaneously.
Program Music	Music intended to describe an event or object.
Ragtime	Compositional style popular at the turn of the century. Usually written for solo piano and characterized by steady pulse with syncopated rhythms.
Renaissance	Musical style period from 1450–1600, characterized by development of the Lutheran chorale and independent instrumental forms, use of a full chromatic scale and full range of voices.
Romantic	Musical style period from 1825–1900, characterized by the development of program music and the influence of nationalism.
Scherzo	Literally "a joke," the term represents a composition of light, playful style often used as a movement in a large composition.
Serialism	A style of composition in which the organization of pitch (or more infrequently any of the other elements of music) is based on a particular form of sequence determined by the composer.
Syllabic	A style of chant in which each syllable of text is assigned only one pitch.
Tone Row	A specific ordering of the twelve chromatic tones.
Twelve Tone Technique	Compositional style based on the use of a tone row and its forty-eight variations. First introduced in the 20th century.
Twentieth Century	Musical style period beginning in 1900 and characterized by percussive sounds, special effects, and electronic sound sources.

STYLE
Vocabulary Worksheet

Part one: Identify true statements with a "T" and false statements with an "F."

____ 1. *Ars nova* and *ars antiqua* are terms describing polyphonic texture.

____ 2. A popular compositional form of the Renaissance Period was *ragtime*.

____ 3. *Twelve tone technique* is a development of the *20th century*.

____ 4. Dividing a melodic line into fragments is called *hocket*.

____ 5. *Ethos* was a philosophy of the ancient Greeks.

Part two: Complete the sentences with the vocabulary word most appropriate.

1. An example of _____ music would be casting dice to determine the pitches of a composition.

2. An accompaniment technique of the Baroque Period consisting of broken chords played by the left hand is called _____.

3. _____ is alternating music between choirs.

4. _____ is a type of monophonic music without regulated rhythm or meter.

5. Characterized by improvised melodies, _____ is a style of music developed in the United States during the early 20th century.

6. A _____ melody is one with a smooth, singing quality.

7. Often a large compositon uses a _____ as one of the movements.

8. Composers of the Romantic Period used _____ to describe events, objects and ideas.

9. Chant is described as _____ when many notes are sung on one syllable.

10. A _____ is a short melody consistently associated with a character or object in a musical work.

Part three: Select the answer that best represents the relationship described.

1. Chamber music to orchestra is like:
   a. road is to highway
   b. strings are to brass
   c. quartet is to choir

2. Impressionism to expressionism is like:
   a. ragtime is to jazz
   b. black is to grey
   c. baroque is to classical

STYLE

Lesson One

Lesson objective: To outline music style periods and discuss Greek influence on the development of music.

Advance preparation: None

Concept statements:

1. The history of music is generally the history of musical styles and forms.

2. Styles and forms of Western music have been categorized under general headings and associated with six general historical time frames: *Medieval* (300-1450); *Renaissance* (1450-1600); *Baroque* (1600-1750); *Classical* (1750-1825); *Romantic* (1825-1900); and *20th Century* (1900-present).

3. The medieval music period is generally associated with the music of the Christian Church, but much of Western music was influenced earlier by the Greeks.

4. The Greeks credited music to the gods and demi-gods of their mythology. To the Greeks, music was closely associated with the pursuit of beauty and truth, and it could be analyzed and understood by applying the principles of mathematics.

5. Eventually the doctrine of *ethos* was developed and music was believed to imitate passions and emotions—anger, courage, lust, sorrow, and so on.

6. According to the ethos doctrine, habitual listening to music of a particular type would eventually cause the listener to develop the character of the music.

7. All music affected character toward traits of (1) serenity and calmness, or (2) excitement and enthusiasm.

8. The great Greek philosophers Plato, Socrates, and Aristotle wanted to censor certain rhythms and modes in order to encourage the characteristics of the "perfect man."

Group activities:

1. Listen to several excerpts from various pieces. *According to the doctrine of ethos*, discuss the emotions and passions ancient Greeks might associate with the examples and why.

Name: _____

STYLE
Lesson One—Assignment One

Part one: Answer each question in short essay form.

1. What relationships between mathematics and music might the ancient Greeks have studied?

2. What experiences have you had with music that relate to the doctrine of ethos?

STYLE, Lesson One—Assignment One *(cont.)*

Part two: According to the doctrine of ethos, identify each musical element as CU = calm and uplifting, or EE = exciting and enthusiastic. Give a brief defense of your opinion.

___ 1. Dissonant harmony

___ 2. Predictable cadences

___ 3. Staccato notes

___ 4. Syncopation

___ 5. Slurred notes

___ 6. Pure intervals

___ 7. Strong accents

___ 8. Obscure cadences

___ 9. Quick tempo

___10. Predictable melody

STYLE

Lesson Two

Lesson objective: To present information regarding the style of music in the Medieval Period.

Advance preparation: Recorded examples of Medieval music.

Concept statements:

Historical Setting

1. Medieval music is associated with the time period of approximately 300 to 1450.

2. This large span of time included such historical events as the fall of the Roman Empire, the rise of European universities, the execution of Joan of Arc, and the expeditions of Marco Polo.

Philosophical Influences

3. During the early part of the Medieval Period, music was almost exclusively linked with the Christian Church and its services. Due to the influence of the church, music was of sacred nature, and melody was always dependent on text taken from religious sources.

4. Music was eventually influenced by shifts in the world's political and educational centers. Sacred music continued to evolve, and secular music was advanced by minstrels and troubadours.

Musical Characteristics

5. Early medieval music was metrically and rhythmically unmeasured, narrow in range, without obvious tonality, and thin in texture. Later melodies have ordered meter and rhythm, and larger skips.

6. Medieval music consisted of single line melodies for many years. Eventually two melodies would be sung simultaneously and the combined motions were described as *oblique*—one melody moves up or down while the other remains on the same pitch; *contrary*—melodies move in opposite directions; or *parallel*—melodies move in the same direction.

7. The practice of combining melodies led to the features now known as polyphony and harmony.

Forms

8. The most prominent form of the Middle Ages was the *Gregorian chant*— a single line melody sung to Latin words; void of strict time values, accent patterns, and apparent tonality; employing a narrow range of notes with rare skips in melody.

9. Chants are described as *syllabic* if most syllables of the text are sung on a single note. *Melismatic* chants are those with long melodic passages sung to a single syllable.

10. Chants were performed in three different ways:
    a. *responsorial*—alternating between soloist and choir,
    b. *antiphonal*—alternating between one choir and another, and
    c. *direct*—without any alternation.

11. During the Medieval Period, three major polyphonic forms were developed:
    a. *organum*—sacred music consisting of a chant part and one or more contrapuntal parts;
    b. *motet*—developed from, and originally quite similar to, four-part organum. New text and melody were combined with an organum chant part already established;
    c. *conductus*—any song of newly composed melody (not borrowed from an established chant) and metrical text on a secular or sacred, but non-liturgical subject.

Significant Influences and Composers

12. During the Medieval Period, *Guido of Arezzo* and *Franco of Cologne* were important figures in the development of music notation. Guido of Arezzo was a medieval music theorist who is often credited with the development of an aid for memorizing pitches in a specific order. Franco of Cologne is credited with the beginning of mensural notation.

13. Important composers of the time include *Leonin*, and *Perotin*, who were also great masters of the Notre Dame school, *Philippe de Vitry*, and *John Dunstable*.

Group activities:

1. Listen to examples of Medieval music and discuss the use or absence of dynamic contrast, range, harmony, texture, rhythm and meter.

2. From your band folder, select a tutti passage of music and divide the class appropriately to play it as antiphonal, direct, or responsorial.

3. Using major and minor scales, devise ways to execute oblique, parallel, and contrary motion.

Name: _____

STYLE
Lesson Two—Assignment One

Part one: Next to each description, write the letter of the appropriate term or person.

____ 1. One note assigned to each syllable.

____ 2. Sacred or secular text to new composed melody.

____ 3. Chant lines alternated between choirs.

____ 4. Single line melody to Latin words, flexible rhythm, non-metrical

____ 5. Masters of Notre Dame school. Medieval composers.

____ 6. Specific line borrowed from organum and developed into independent form.

____ 7. Many notes for a single syllable of text.

____ 8. Credited with early systems of notation.

____ 9. Composers of the medieval period.

____10. Polyphonic, sacred text.

a. antiphonal
b. conductus
c. Leonin and Perotin
d. Organum
e. Gregorian chant

f. de Vitry and Dunstable
g. syllabic
h. Franco de Cologne and Guido de Arezzo
i. motet
j. melismatic

Part two: Identify the melodic motion within the circles as O = oblique, C = contrary, or P = parallel.

©1998 by Parker Publishing Company, Inc.

STYLE, Lesson Two—Assignment One *(cont.)*

Part three: Write a melody for the following text in each of the forms named.

Benedictus qui venit (Blessed is He that cometh)

GREGORIAN CHANT
syllabic

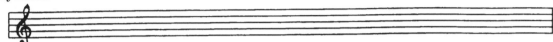

melismatic

ORGANUM
oblique motion

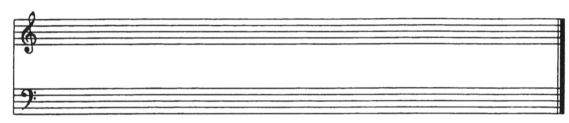

parallel motion

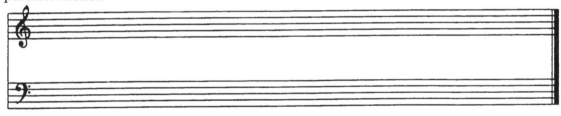

contrary

STYLE

Lesson Three

Lesson objective: To present information regarding the style of music in the Renaissance Period.

Advance preparation: Recorded examples of Renaissance music.

Concept statements:

Historical Setting

1. The *Renaissance Period* is associated with the time frame 1450 to 1600.

2. During this time period, Columbus sailed to America, Michelangelo painted the ceiling of the Sistine Chapel, Cortez conquered Mexico, and Gutenburg developed *movable metal type*.

Philosophical Influences

3. The "age of the Renaissance" promoted the idea of "rebirth." Thoughts were on reviving the glories of the golden age of ancient Greece and Rome.

4. Educational focus broadened to include secular study as well as religious. Artists and writers strove to make their works pleasing to men as well as God.

5. Martin Luther initiated a religious reformation that broadened music's role in church services.

Musical Characteristics

6. During the Renaissance Period, the music culture experienced tremendous growth. More music was composed than in any previous era.

7. Composers began to produce music intended for aesthetic fulfillment as well as practicality.

8. Renaissance music was conceived in parts, and emphasis was placed on pleasing combinations of sound.

9. For the first time music employed the entire chromatic scale, a full range of voices, and instruments in several independent forms, and vocal text expanded from Latin and poetry to all forms of literature.

Forms

10. Vocal forms that flourished during the Renaissance Period include the *madrigal*, *aria*, *chanson*, and *Lutheran chorale*.

11. The style and performance of instrumental music was similar to vocal music, but several independent forms were developed including the *canzona*, *variation*, *toccatta*, *fugue* and *suite*.

12. During the Renaissance Period a great number and variety of instruments were used. Ensembles were generally arranged in groups of like instruments to achieve a uniform timbre.

Significant Influences and Composers

13. Prominent influences and composers of the Renaissance include *Palestrina*, *Orlando de Lasso*, *William Byrd*, *Josquin de Prez* and the development of *movable type printing*.

Group activity:
1. Listen to samples of Renaissance music and discuss its difference and likeness to medieval and modern music.

STYLE
Lesson Three—Assignment One

Part one: Fill in the blanks to correctly complete each statement.

1. The time frame associated with the Renaissance style period is _____ to _____.

2. Three historical, but nonmusical events of the Renaissance era were _____, _____, and _____.

3. Key words to describe the prominent philosophical influences of the Renaissance era are _____, and _____.

4. Two musical characteristics of the Renaissance era are _____ and _____.

5. Important compositional forms of the Renaissance Period include _____ and _____.

Part two: Prepare a brief essay to answer the following questions. Use reference materials available in school or public libraries.

1. What is the meaning of "Renaissance" and in what way is the term represented by the attitude, musical performance, and composition of the time?

STYLE, Lesson Three—Assignment One *(cont.)*

2. Who were some prominent Renaissance composers from Spain, Germany, and England and what were their specific musical contributions?

3. What was the importance of movable type printing to music? Who and what were the influences in its development?

Part three: Listen to a recording of a Renaissance piece and describe it according to the following format.

TITLE	COMPOSER
PERFORMANCE MEDIUM	RHYTHM
TEXTURE	HARMONY
DYNAMICS	MELODY

STYLE

Lesson Four

Lesson objective: To present information regarding music of the Baroque Period.

Advance preparation: Recorded examples of Baroque music.

Concept statements:

Historical Setting

1. The Baroque Period is associated with the time frame 1600 to 1750.

2. Historical events of this era include the arrival of the Mayflower, the printing of the first book in the English colonies—*The Bay Psalm Book*, and the reign of Peter the Great.

Philosophical Influences

3. The Baroque era was a time of profound change in the way men thought of the world and its laws of reason and logic.

4. Science, the arts, and philosophy were advanced by individuals such as Shakespeare, Milton, Rembrandt, Descartes, Newton, Francis Bacon, and Galileo.

Musical Characteristics

5. Composers employed a vocabulary of specific musical figures and devices to represent the affections or "states of the soul" (rage, heroism, grandeur, wonder and so on), and to intensify music effects by means of extreme contrasts.

6. Composers also began to write for specific performance mediums (e.g., solo voice with lute accompaniment, violin trio, four voices, and so on). Prior to this time, compositions were written without anticipation of a particular performance idiom.

7. Ultimately during the Baroque Period a complex system of music classification and distinctions developed between music of three types: *theatrical*, *church*, and *concert* or *chamber*.

8. During the Baroque era, music began to be written and heard in measures defined by patterns of strong and weak beats.

9. A prominent characteristic of the Baroque era was the *basso continuo*. This was a strong and uncluttered bass part that dictated the harmonic progression of the entire piece. Eventually the basso continuo shifted musical direction from counterpoint to homophony.

Forms

10. Important forms of the Baroque Period include *passacaglia, suite, chaconne, oratorio*, and *opera*.

Significant Influences and Composers

11. The *equal temperament system* was developed during the Baroque era and reflected the advancement of instrumental music as an independent idiom.

12. Prominent composers of the Baroque Period include *J. S. Bach, Vivaldi, Scarlatti, Handel*, and *Purcell*.

Group activities:

1. Discuss the Baroque categories of church, theatrical, and chamber music. Could such defined divisions be applied to music of today?

2. Listen to both a vocal and instrumental piece from the Baroque era. Discuss what musical devices were used to express the meaning of the text in the vocal piece, and what devices were used to represent a "state of soul" in the instrumental piece.

3. Listen to the *Chaconne* from the *Holst Suite in E♭*. Identify the basso continuo.

STYLE
Lesson Four—Assignment One

Part one: Fill in the blanks to correctly complete each statement.

1. The time frame associated with the Baroque style period is _____ to _____.

2. Three historical, but nonmusical events of the Baroque era were _____, _____, and _____.

3. Prominent philosophers and scientists of the Baroque Period include _____, and _____.

4. Two musical characteristics of the Baroque era are _____ and _____.

5. Important compositional forms of the Baroque period include _____ and _____.

Part two: Assume the philosophy of a Baroque musician that music is intended to represent ideas and affections. Name and describe music pieces or passages that, *for you*, represent the following:

	Music Title	Description
1. Spring weather		
2. Fireworks		
3. Torment		
4. Lost love		
5. Drooping wings		

STYLE, Lesson Four—Assignment One *(cont.)*

Part three: Write a short essay answer for each of the following questions. Use library reference materials as needed.

1. What are three prominent compositions by George F. Handel and what characteristics illustrate the Baroque musical style?

2. What is homophony and how did basso continuo contribute to its development?

3. What were some changes in thought initiated by the philosophers and scientists of the Baroque Period (Francis Bacon, Galileo, Newton) and how did they influence music of that era?

STYLE

Lesson Five

Lesson objective: To present information regarding music of the Classical Period.

Advance preparation: Recorded examples of music of the Classical music period.

Concept statements:

Historical Setting

1. The classical period is associated with the time frame of 1750 to 1825.

2. During this time, the American and French Revolutions began and ended. Watts patented the steam engine, and the metronome was invented.

Philosophical Influences

3. The classical era was known as the "age of enlightenment." Initially this concept fostered negativism and criticism, but eventually skepticism gave way to the idea that the common natural instincts of man were the source of truth. The new faith in the individual was reflected in a German literary movement known as *Storm and Stress.*

4. Throughout Europe, the restrictions of national boundaries and social status gave way to a cosmopolitan ideal and a push for equality.

5. The arts, science, literature and philosophy all began to take into account the general public and not just noblemen and public figures.

Musical Characteristics

6. Music of the Classical Period broke from the practice of focusing on a principal theme and began introducing contrast within a movement or theme itself.

7. Gradual dynamic changes replaced the writing of the abrupt, terraced dynamics of the Baroque era.

8. Melodies tended to solidify into distinct phrases of two or four measures and thereby establish clear periodic structures.

9. A common musical feature of the era was the *alberti bass*—an accompaniment figure of repeating notes of a broken chord.

Form

10. Three instrumental forms served as the foundation of Classical music style—the *sonata, solo concerto*, and *symphony*. These forms of the Classical era became models for art music of subsequent eras.

Significant Influences and Composers

   11. Prominent composers of the classical period were *Haydn, Scarlatti, Mozart,* and the young *Beethoven*.

Group activities:

   1. Listen to examples of Classical music and note occurrences of alberti bass and crescendo/decrescendo.

   2. If the lessons regarding musical form have been presented, review the outline of the sonata.

Name: _____

STYLE
Lesson Five—Assignment One

Part one: Fill in the blanks to correctly complete each statement.

1. The time frame associated with the Classical style period is _____ to _____.

2. Three historical, but nonmusical events of the Classical era were _____, _____, and _____.

3. Key words used to describe prominent philosophies of the Classical Period include _____, and _____.

4. Two musical characteristics of the Classical era are _____ and _____.

5. Important compositional forms of the Classical Period include _____ and _____.

Part two: For each of the composers listed, name three characteristic works.

Scarlatti

1.

2.

3.

Mozart

1.

2.

3

Gluck

1.

2.

3.

STYLE, Lesson Five—Assignment One *(cont.)*

Haydn

1.

2.

3.

Beethoven

1.

2.

3.

Part three: Select and listen to three of the compositions cited in *Part one*. Give the title of the pieces and describe each according to the following characteristics:

Dynamics (unchanging, subtle, extreme . . .)

Harmony (chordal, arpeggiated, dissonant, consonant . . .)

Melody (intervals, range, embellishments . . .)

Texture (polyphony, homophony, small ensemble, orchestra . . .)

1.

2.

3.

STYLE

Lesson Six

Lesson objective: To present information regarding music of the Romantic Period.

Advance preparation: Recorded examples of music of the Romantic Period.

Concept statements:

Historical Setting

1. The Romantic style period is associated with the time frame of 1825 to 1900.

2. This was the era of the industrial revolution and Darwin's *Theory of Evolution*. Historical events include the assassination of Lincoln, the first use of electricity, telegraph, and phonograph.

Philosophical Influences

3. The philosophy influencing all art forms of the nineteenth century was one of remoteness, strangeness, boundlessness—transcending immediate occasions to "seize eternity."

4. Many prominent composers of the Romantic era were very articulate and became intrigued with literary expression. They bridged the apparent gap between literature and pure instrumental music with the concept of *program music.*

Musical Characteristics

5. Program music was intended to "transmute" subject matter to the imagination of the listeners by way of large chords, lyrical melodies, elusive cadences, many accents, and chromatic harmonies.

6. *Nationalism* was also a distinguishing factor of Romantic music. The folk songs of countries came to be the chief thematic material in works characterizing the national style.

7. Dynamic changes were taken to extreme, and an effect of "swelling" sound was prevalent.

Forms

8. During the Romantic Period, many classical forms continued to be popular. Among the new forms that were introduced are: *grand opera, music drama,* and *symphonic poem.*

9. The symphonic poem was actually a type of program music. It was generally a composition of only one movement and represented in sound, events of national life or scenes from a landscape.

156

Significant Influences and Composers

10. During the latter part of the Romantic Period, the term *impressionism* (a term borrowed from the visual art of the time) was ascribed to a group of composers. Among them were: *Debussy, Ravel, De Falla,* and *Respighi.*

11. Composers associated with the nationalistic style of the Romantic Period include: *Wagner, Tchaikovsky, Mussorgsky, Dvorak, Greig,* and *Richard Strauss.*

12. Other equally prominent composers of the time were: *Brahms, Faure, Irving Berlin, Ives,* and *Berlioz.*

Group activities:

1. Listen to examples of Romantic style music and discuss the characteristics of harmony, melody, texture, tone color, tonality, and so on.

2. Select two pieces representative of the nationalistic style but by different composers. Listen to both examples without telling the class the composers' names or nationalities. Try to identify features that distinguish one piece from the other.

3. If possible, play through a program piece from the Romantic era and discuss the features that most effectively represent the subject of the composition.

Name: _____

STYLE
Lesson Six—Assignment One

Part one: Fill in the blanks to correctly complete each statement.

1. The time frame associated with the Romantic style period is _____ to _____.

2. Three historical but nonmusical events of the Romantic era were _____, _____, and _____.

3. Key words used to describe prominent philosophies of the Romantic era are _____ and _____.

4. Compositions of the Romantic Period followed three "routes": nationalism, _____, and _____.

5. Phrases descriptive of Romantic Period music are: _____ melodies, _____ harmonies, and _____ dynamics.

Part two: Use library reference materials to complete this section.

1. Name and briefly describe two examples of program music.

A.

B.

2. List two composers associated with the nationalistic music style and give a brief biographical sketch of each.

A.

B.

©1998 by Parker Publishing Company, Inc.

STYLE, Lesson Six—Assignment One *(cont.)*

Part three: Write a brief essay in response to two of the following questions.

1. How would the invention of electricity and the phonograph affect the history of music?

2. How are the features of impressionistic art related to music of that description?

3. What influences might have caused the rise of a nationalistic style of music?

STYLE

Lesson Seven

Lesson objective: To present information regarding music of the Twentieth Century Period.

Advance preparation: Recorded examples of Twentieth Century style music.

Concept statements:

Historical Setting

1. The twentieth century thus far has seen transportation develop from cars to planes to spacecraft. Communication has progressed from telegraph to satellite and phonograph to laser disc. International relations have swung from diplomatic tension to horrific world wars to abdication of prominent powers and geographical barriers.

Philosophical Influences

2. The philosophies of the twentieth century have been reflected in various movements including work programs of the Depression, equal rights of minorities, women, and gays, anti-war demonstrations, and the arms race.

3. It is impossible to isolate any one single philosophical influence of the twentieth century, but the worldwide trend of thought can very generally be divided into two parts: pre-war tension, rebellion and unshackled experimentation: post-war attempts at adjustment of morals, politics, society and economics.

Musical Characteristics

4. Art music of the twentieth century has pursued three general trends: (1) the continuation of nationalistic, folk idiom attributes, (2) new musical discoveries applied to established forms and techniques of the past, and (3) the twelve-tone composition style called *dodecaphonic*.

5. The new sounds of the twentieth century include: jagged contour; mixed meters, tonalities, and rhythms; extreme contrasts; percussive sounds; special effects; atonality (without tonal center); new sound sources including electronics and the return of polyphony.

Forms

6. The twentieth century has been a time of renewed interest in the musical forms of the Classical and Baroque eras, as well as development of new forms such as jazz, electronic music, *tone row* or *serial music*, *musique concrete*, and *aleatory*.

7. A tone row is a form of serial music in which a set of the twelve tones are arranged in any random sequence (as determined by the composer), and then written in retrograde, inversion, and retrograde inversion. Each of the four forms (original, retrograde, inversion, and retrograde inversion) is then transposed to start on each of the other eleven tones. The result is a matrix of 48 forms of the original row and the composer uses the notes as rows in his composition. The resultant work is completely void of tonality or conventional pitch association. Some composers have developed ways to serialize rhythm, dynamics, and timbre.

8. Musique concrete is a compositional style characterized by the use of tape recorded sounds and noises and the avoidance of traditional instruments.

9. Aleatory music is that in which the composer invites elements of chance into the performance or the composition. Some examples of this principle are throwing dice to determine the pitches used, or writing pitches, but leaving the performer to determine their order of appearance.

Significant Influences and Composers

10. Composers of the twentieth century, including every style and idiom, are: *Vaughan Williams, Stravinsky, Chance, Shostakovich, Gershwin, Joplin, Copland, Webern, Schoenberg, Elgar, Bartok, Hindemith, Holst,* and *Piston*.

Group activities:

1. Compose a tone row for the class and as a class, complete a matrix by writing the row in all its transpositions, retrogrades, and inversions. Assign each row of the matrix a number to indicate sequence of performance and play through each row on a predetermined rhythm.

2. Rehearse a jazz, ragtime, or blues composition. Discuss the influences that led to the development of that particular style.

3. Invite a guest to class who can demonstrate electronic music and the compositional aids available through computers.

Name: _____

STYLE
Lesson Seven—Assignment One

Part one: Fill in the blanks to correctly complete each statement.

1. The Twentieth Century music style period followed the _____ style period.

2. Historical events of the 20th century include _____, _____, _____, and _____.

3. Technological developments of the 20th century have made music readily available to the public. Two examples of such developments are _____, and _____.

4. Twelve-tone row compositional style is called _____.

5. Compositional style which involves chance in some aspect is called _____.

Part two: Write a brief essay in response to the following questions.

1. What were some of the popular American songs of the WWI, WWII, or Vietnam eras and how do these songs reflect the common American attitudes of the time?

STYLE, Lesson Seven—Assignment One *(cont.)*

2. What are some compositions by Aaron Copland, and how are they a continuation of the nationalistic, folk idiom of America?

Part three: List two prominent composers and two of their compositions exemplary of each 20th century art music trend.

1. Continuation of nationalistic, folk idiom attributes.

A.

B.

2. New musical discoveries applied to established forms and techniques.

A.

B.

3. Twelve tone row; dodecaphonic composition.

A.

B.

STYLE
Lesson Seven—Assignment Two

Part one: Use a cassette recorder to tape ten sounds not intended as musical performances. Note the sounds and sources.

1.

2.

3.

4.

5.

6.

7.

©1998 by Parker Publishing Company, Inc.

STYLE, Lesson Seven—Assignment Two *(cont.)*

8.

9.

10.

Part two: Use multi-tapes and recorders to organize the ten recorded sounds into a "musique concrete" composition.

Name: _____

STYLE
Unit Quiz

Part one: Fill in the boxes of the table with the letters representing appropriate information from the list on the next page. There may be more than one letter in each box. Headings are; *time frame, music period, historical setting, philosophical influences, musical characteristics, forms introduced* and *influentual composers.*

time frame	music period	hist. setting	philos. infl.	music char.	forms intro.	infl. comp.
1.						
2.						
3.						
4.						
5.						
6.						

a. Columbus to America, movable type printing, Martin Luther's reformation.

b. storm and stress, enlightenment, cosmopolitan

c. 1825-1900

d. Descartes, Bacon, Shakespeare, Rembrandt

e. Classical

f. percussive sounds, special effects, serialism, atonality

g. ethos

h. 1450-1600

i. Vivaldi, Bach, Handel, equal temperament

j. Haydn, Mozart, Gluck, early Beethoven

k. jazz, folk idioms, aleatory

l. Renaissance

m. Holst, Vaughn Williams, Stravinsky

n. chants, psalms, mass

o. phrases, tonality, variation in movements, alberti bass

p. Boethius, Leonin

q. 300-1450

r. passacaglia, fugue, concerto grosso, toccatta.

s. Romantic

t. Guido, Machaut, notation

u. large chords, sound color, elusive cadences

v. motet, organum, conductus

w. 1600-1750

x. Debussy, Brahms, Berlioz

y. basso continuo, musical devices—"states of the soul"

z. Twentieth Century

aa. Medieval

bb. full chromatic scale and voice range, more than Latin

cc. sonata, symphony, solo concerto

dd. Martin, Palestrina, W. Byrd

ee. industrial revolution, Darwin, Lincoln assassinated.

ff. American colonization, *Bay Psalm Book*, Peter the Great

gg. program music, boundless, transcending, remote

hh. 1750-1825

ii. TV, radio, technology

jj. Beethoven, Chopin, Schubert

kk. Josquin de Prez, Monteverdi

ll. Copland, Schoenberg

mm. Baroque

nn. order, non-metrical, modal

oo. WWI and WWII, Vietnam

pp. accompanied vocal, madrigal, similar tone colors

qq. 1900 - present

rr. American/French revolutions, steam engine

ss. grand opera, drama, symphonic poem

tt. Aristotle, Plato, early Christianity, Joan of Arc

uu. instrumental groups, canzona

vv. interest in antiquity, "rebirth"

STYLE Unit Quiz (cont.)

Part two: Select five of the following terms and define and describe them as they relate to music and time period.

1. Basso continuo

2. Secular

3. Reformation (M. Luther)

4. Antiphonal

5. Serialism

6. Ethos

7. Program music

8. Organum

9. Alberti bass

10. Homophonic

Part three: Answer two of the following questions in essay form.

1. What influence did Beethoven have in two distinct musical style periods?

2. What were some major points of development between single lines of chant and multimedia, large group works of today?

3. What are some of the influences that affect your involvement as a listener, performer, student, and composer of music today? Are any of the influences similar to those experienced before in music history? If so, in what ways?

Unit Six

FORM

Form Vocabulary List

Form Vocabulary Worksheet

Lesson One

(1) To present the notion of form in all compositions and the principles and procedures to look for in analysis. (2) To introduce basic form mapping procedures.

Lesson Two

To present the various binary forms—two reprise, bar form, inverted bar form, simple and rounded.

Lesson Three

To introduce ternary form.

Lesson Four

To present the outline of fugal form and describe the fugal devices: Stretto, mirror, augmentation and diminution.

Lesson Five

(1) To present and describe the sonata allegro and sonatina compositional forms. (2) To explain the relationship of sonata allegro form to the *concert-overture*.

Lesson Six

To introduce the five- and seven-part rondo forms.

Lesson Seven

To present eight possible forms of sectional variation.

Lesson Eight

To define ostinato and to introduce two types of continuous variation forms—the passacaglia and the chaconne.

Form Unit Quiz

FORM
Vocabulary List

Answer In fugal procedure, the imitation(s) of the original statement of the theme or subject.

Antecedent The first phrase of a melodic period.

Augmentation Imitation of a subject in proportionally larger duration values.

Bridge A passage serving to join two themes or sections.

Canon A contrapuntal device whereby a subject is imitated in its entirety in one or more voices.

Coda A final or concluding passage.

Consequent The reply, or answer to an antecedent.

Countersubject Thematic material introduced in a fugue but unrelated to the subject.

Dependent Transition A passage linking themes or sections—dependent in that it contains material from the preceding theme or section.

Development A procedure and a section wherein thematic material is expounded.

Diminution Imitation of a subject in proportionally smaller duration values.

Episode A portion of fugue that does not contain a statement of the subject.

Exposition A portion of a fugue and of a sonata allegro wherein the subject or themes are fully introduced.

Independent Transition A passage linking two themes or sections, but composed of material not related to preceding themes.

Overture A particular genre of composition which often follows the outline of a sonata allegro.

Real Answer The exact intervalic imitation of a subject.

Recapitulation The section of a sonata or sonatina wherein the themes are restated in their entirety and original sequence.

Retransition A passage linking sections previously presented or, the latter portion of the development section of a sonata allegro leading back to original keys.

Retrograde The imitation of a subject in reverse.

Stretto	A fugal device whereby answers begin before the completion of the subject.
Subject	The initial statement of a fugal theme.
Suite	A work consisting of several movements of varying, but related character.
Symphony	A large instrumental form consisting of three or four movements in fairly standardized form.
Toccata	A compositional genre usually characterized by full chords and running passages.
Tonal Answer	An imitation that varies intervals of the subject.
Transition	A passage connecting two themes or sections.
Trio	A segment of composition played between significant sections of a march, or minuet movement of a sonata. Characterized by a change in instrumentation, dynamic, style or meter.

Name: _____

FORM
Vocabulary Worksheet

Part one: Identify each statement with a "T" for true and an "F" for false.

___ 1. Within the *exposition* of a sonata allegro, all themes are fully introduced.

___ 2. A *tonal answer* is a near exact imitation of the subject, with some differences in intervals.

___ 3. A *trio* is a large section of a fugue wherein no subject is stated completely.

___ 4. Some compositions end with a passage of finality called *overture*.

___ 5. A group of related but varied movements is called a *suite*.

Part two: Complete each sentence with the most appropriate vocabulary word

1. In a fugue, the _____ is the first statement of the theme.

2. A fugal imitation at the dominant level, but intervalically exact is called a _____.

3. Imitating an eighth note as a quarter, a quarter as a half, and a half note as a whole is an example of _____.

4. A transition consisting of material from a preceding theme or section is called _____.

5. A _____ is a common section in a march—characterized by a change in instrumentation, dynamic, style or meter.

Part three: Select the answer that best represents the relationship described.

1. Antecedent to consequent is like:
    a. hypothesis is to theory
    b. question is to answer
    c. tadpole is to frog

2. Retrograde to 1-2-3-4 is like:
    a. N-O-P-Q is to J-K-L-M
    b. A-B-C-D is to Z-Y-X-W
    c. M-L-K-J is to J-K-L-M

3. Exposition to development to recapitulation is like:
    a. wood to primer to paint
    b. title to text to summary
    c. sun to window to curtain

©1998 by Parker Publishing Company, Inc.

FORM

Lesson One

Lesson objectives: (1) To present the notion of form in all compositions and the principles and procedures to look for in analysis. (2) To introduce basic form mapping procedures.

Advance preparation: None

Concept statements:

1. All the elements of music combine to give compositions *form*.

2. All compositions are based on the principles of *unity* and *variety*. Form analysis is determining how and where compositions employ these principles.

3. A diagram outlining a composition's unity and variety can be called a *form map* and shows the composition's overall shape.

4. Many compositions have followed generally similar shapes. Groups of similarly shaped compositions are categorized as particular form types, some of which are: *rondo, binary and ternary, sonata allegro*, and *fugue*.

5. All compositions use procedures of *repetition, contrast, variation* or *development*. Through listening for these procedures and the placement of final cadences, large sections of a composition can be identified.

6. A form map uses a horizontal arc to represent each large section of a composition:

7. Where two arcs meet, the measure number is given and the cadence is identified. Under each arc, there are descriptions of that particular section. Sections are identified with letters to illustrate unity or contrast:

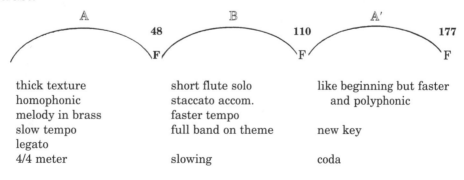

A	B	A'
thick texture	short flute solo	like beginning but faster
homophonic	staccato accom.	and polyphonic
melody in brass	faster tempo	
slow tempo	full band on theme	new key
legato		
4/4 meter	slowing	coda

175

8. More detailed analysis shows smaller sections, phrases, keys, and specific measures:

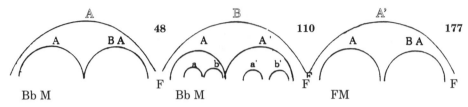

thick texture	short flute solo	like beginning but faster
homophonic	staccato accom.	and polyphonic
melody in brass	faster tempo	
slow tempo	full band on theme	new key
legato		
4/4 meter	slowing	coda

Group activities:

1. Play through a composition from your band folder and identify the large sections. Discuss the principles of unity and variety as they apply to the large sections.

2. Play through parts of a composition one phrase at a time and discuss the procedures of contrast, variety, repetition, and development.

3. Make a form map of one of the compositions from your band folder.

Name: _____

FORM
Lesson One—Assignment One

Part one: Considering the principles of unity and variety, label the sections and subsections of the following familiar song. Write a brief paragraph defending your choice of labels.

Old McDonald had a farm, ee-i, ee-i, oh. And on this farm he had a dog. ee-i, ee-i, oh.

With a bark bark here, and a bark bark there. Here a bark, there a bark, everywhere a bark bark.

Old McDonald had a farm, ee-i, ee-i, oh.

Part two: Make a form map of a band piece (or section), rehearsed in class this week. Include the composition title, section labels, important measure numbers, general descriptions of sections, key changes, and cadence points.

FORM

Lesson Two

Lesson objective: To present the various binary forms—two reprise, bar form, inverted bar form, simple and rounded.

Advance preparation: Use Appendix 4: "Band Compositions by Form" to identify and locate a recording of a binary form composition.

Concept statements:

1. *Binary* form is a two-part composition. Traditionally the two parts are labeled "𝔸" and "𝔹."

2. The labels 𝔸 and 𝔹 represent contrasting sections of a composition, but all binary forms are *simple* or *rounded* depending on how the sections relate to each other.

3. *Simple binary form* consists of independent sections 𝔸 and 𝔹, with no material from 𝔸 in section 𝔹.

4. *Rounded binary form* consists of sections 𝔸 and 𝔹, but within 𝔹 there is a return of material from 𝔸 . Section 𝔹 is not completely independent; it serves as a bridge between the original 𝔸 and the return of 𝔸 material.

5. Simple or rounded binary forms may be further distinguished as *two reprise, bar,* or *inverted bar* forms.

6. When both 𝔸 and 𝔹 sections repeat, the composition is identified as two reprise binary form (simple or rounded.)

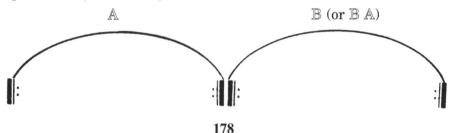

178

7. When only section 𝔸 repeats, the composition is identified as bar binary form (simple or rounded.)

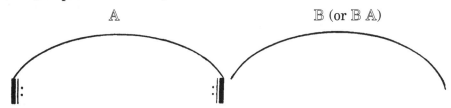

8. When only section 𝔹 repeats, the composition is identified as inverted bar binary form (simple or rounded.)

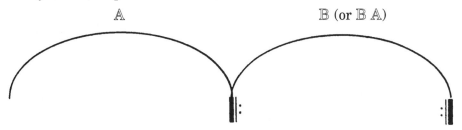

Group activities:
1. Listen to the example of a binary composition. Identify it as simple or rounded and two-part, bar or inverted bar form.

2. From your band folder select a piece that has two adjacent contrasting sections of any length. Manipulate the sections to form two reprise, bar and inverted bar forms.

Name: _____

FORM
Lesson Two—Assignment One

Part one: Draw a map of simple binary, inverted bar form. Include section labels, important cadence points, and repeat signs.

Part two: Describe the changes necessary to the map in *Part one* to map a rounded binary, bar form—then two reprise form.

FORM

Lesson Three

Lesson objective: To introduce ternary form.

Advance preparation: Use Appendix 4: "Band Composition Titles by Form" to identify and locate a recording of a composition in ternary form.

Concept statements:

1. *Ternary* form consists of three large and distinct sections.
2. The sections are traditionally labeled A B A, A A′ A″, or A B C, depending on the contrast or similarity between sections.
3. Within each large section of a ternary form, there will be a one-part form or a binary form.

Group activities:

1. Listen to the example of ternary form as many times as is necessary to identify the major sections and determine their proper labels.
2. Refer to the form map while listening to one section at a time. Write in measure numbers, phrases, cadence types and identify one- or two-part forms within each section.

FORM
Lesson Three—Assignment One

Part one: Draw a map of a ternary form. Show three possible section labels.

FORM

Lesson Four

Lesson objectives: To present the outline of fugal form and describe the fugal devices stretto, mirror, augmentation, and diminution.

Advance preparation: Be prepared with a recording of a fugue and a familiarity with its basic structure. Identify examples of fugal devices used in music from your band folder.

Concept statements:

1. The term *fugue* represents a general compositional form as well as a contrapuntal procedure.

2. The procedure of a fugue is to introduce a short melody called the *subject*—stated at the beginning of the piece by one voice only and imitated by other voices in short succession throughout the piece.

3. The first imitation of the subject is called the *answer* and is stated at the dominant level, i. e., at the interval a fifth above or a fourth below the subject.

4. Fugal answers are of two types: a *real answer* is an exact imitation of the subject at the dominant level; a *tonal answer* is near exact imitation, but with slight variation from the intervals of the subject.

5. In fugue form, a section is labeled the *exposition* when all voices have stated the subject.

6. The exposition is followed by a section called the *episode* wherein are heard *fragments* of the subject and other contrapuntal material which modulates into a new key.

7. The full statement of subject and answer in a new key marks the end of the fugue's first large section and the beginning of a new section called *middle entry*. In this section one or two voices drops out, but counterpoint continues and an episode follows an exposition much as in the first section.

8. A third and *final section* is marked by the return of all voices in counterpoint stating subject, answer, or fragments thereof to the the end of the piece.

9. An example of a fugue form follows:

FIRST SECTION
EXPOSITION   EPISODE

Sop.   answer′   #############   *continued counterpoint*
                                                                 fragments of subject
Alto   subject   ///   *modulation to new key*

Tenor   answer‴   &&

Bass   answer″   **********

MIDDLE ENTRY
                                                                         EPISODE
Sop.

Alto

Tenor   *etc.*

          subject   ```
Bass
                    answer   ~~~~~~~~~~~~~~

FINAL SECTION

Sop. ⎫
Alto ⎬
Tenor ⎬   all voices in to the end
Bass ⎭

10. Often fugal devices are used within non-fugal compositional forms.
    Examples of fugal devices are:

    a. *Stretto*—the imitation of a subject before the subject is completed.
        Sometimes all the voices are simultaneously stating parts of the subject,
        thus causing a layered or *strata* effect.

    b. *Mirror*—a subject that can be answered in melodic inversion, in reverse
        pitch order called *retrograde*, or both. As if reading the notes in a mirror.

    c. *Augmentation*—imitation of the subject in proportionally larger duration
        values.

    d. *Diminution*—imitation of the subject in proportionally smaller duration
        values.

Group activities:

    1. Listen to a fugal piece and identify the subject, answers, exposition,
        episodes, and large sections.

    2. Play passages of music from your band folder and identify fugal devices.

    3. Select a short unison phrase of band music and play it as mirror,
        augmented and diminuted imitation.

FORM
Lesson Four—Assignment One

Part one: Draw a map of fugue form. Include section labels, exposition and episode portions, subject and answers, and important descriptive characteristics, such as, one or two voices out, all voices in, possible episode, new key, and so on.

©1998 by Parker Publishing Company, Inc.

Part two: Name and describe three fugal devices.

1.

2.

3.

185

FORM, Lesson Four—Assignment One *(cont.)*

Part three: Arrange the familiar song "Row, Row, Row the Boat" into a fugue in four voices. Use at least one occurrence each of stretto, retrograde, and inverted imitation.

FORM

Lesson Five

Lesson objectives: (1) To present and describe the sonata allegro and sonatina compositional forms. (2) To explain the relationship of sonata allegro form to the *concert-overture*.

Advance preparation: Have a recording of a piece to illustrate sonata allegro.

Concept statements:

1. *Sonata allegro* is a name descriptive of the first movement, or *allegro*, of a full sonata. It is a type of *ternary* form that developed from the *two reprise* form.

2. The three sections of a sonanta allegro are labeled *exposition, development,* and *recapitulation*.

3. Within the exposition section a *principal theme, subordinate theme,* and *closing theme* are presented.

4. The principal and subordinate themes are separated by a *transition*. A transition is further classified as *dependent* if it consists of material from the principal theme or *independent* if it consists of new melodic material. The transition serves to move the composition from the tonic key of the principal theme to the dominant key used for the subordinate theme.

5. The closing theme in the exposition continues in the dominant key and is followed by a small "tag" or "tail" called a *codetta*.

6. Within the development section, melodic material from the themes is manipulated by techniques such as imitation, sequence, and modulation in order to bring the composition back to the tonic key.

7. The latter part of the development section leads back to the original themes in the tonic key. This portion is referred to as the *retransition*.

8. The final section, or recapitulation, of the sonata allegro form presents each theme again, this time in the tonic key to the end. The closing theme is followed by a full coda or final cadence.

9. Sonata allegro form can be diagrammed as follows:

EXPOSITION	DEVELOPMENT retransition	RECAPITULATION
P.T. trans. S. T. C. T. codetta	*development of melodic material from expos.*	P. T. trans. S. T. C. T. coda
I _ _ I ~ ~ ~ ~ V _ _ _ _ V	V _ _ _ _ _ _ _ _ _ _ _ _ _ _ V	I _ _ _ _ I ~ ~ ~ I _ _ _ _ _ _ _ I
i _ _ i ~ ~ ~ ~ III _ _ _ _ III	III _ _harm. movement to_ _V	i _ _ _ _ i ~ ~ ~ I _ _I i _ _ _ i

10. *Sonatina* form is exactly like the sonata allegro, but does not include a development section. Instead, the exposition is followed by a very short melodic *bridge*. A bridge serves the same purpose as a transition, but joins sections instead of themes:

EXPOSITION		RECAPITULATION
P.T. trans. S. T. C. T. codetta	*no development section* *very short bridge*	P. T. trans. S. T. C. T. coda
I _ _ _ I ~ ~ ~ ~V _ _ _ _ _V i _ _ _ i ~ ~ ~ ~III _ _ _ _III		I _ _ _ _ I~ ~ ~ I_ _ _ _ _ _ _ _ _I i _ _ _ _ i~ ~ ~ I_ _I i _ _ _ _ _ _i

11. Many band overtures fit the sonata allegro form and are properly classified as *concert overtures*.

Group activities:

1. Listen to an example of a composition in sonata allegro form. Identify the principal, subordinate, and closing themes. Diagram the large sections and discuss what devices are used to develop the themes in the development sections.

2. Analyze the use of transitions and bridges in music from your band folder. Determine if the transitions are dependent or independent.

Name: _____

FORM
Lesson Five—Assignment One

Part one: Draw a map of sonata allegro form. Include section labels, themes, transitions, and key changes.

Part two: Describe the changes necessary to the map in *Part one* to show sonatina form.

FORM

Lesson Six

Lesson objective: To introduce the five- and seven-part rondo forms.

Advance preparation: Have a recording of a five- or seven-part rondo composition.

Concept statements:

1. A *five-part rondo* is made up of five sections of 𝔸, 𝔹, and ℂ material.
2. Transitions and retransitions are used between sections—transitions lead to new material, retransitions lead to material previously presented.
3. Each section is in a key different, but related to the segment preceding it.
4. A possible example of a five-part rondo form follows:

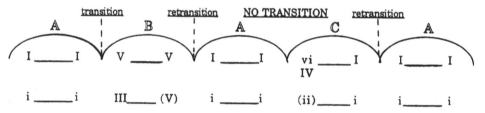

5. A seven-part rondo follows generally the same format of the five-part rondo except 𝔸′ and 𝔹′ sections are added:

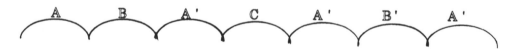

Group activity:
1. Listen to a composition in rondo form and identify the sections, transitions, and retransitions.

190

Name: _____

FORM
Lesson Six—Assignment One

Part one: Draw a map of a five-part rondo form. Include section labels, transitions, retransitions, and important key changes.

Part two: Describe alternative section labels possible on the map in *Part one* and the changes they necessitate in transitions and retransitions.

FORM

Lesson Seven

Lesson objective: To present eight possible forms of sectional variation.

Advance preparation: Have a recording of a composition in sectional variation form.

Concept statements:

1. In *sectional variations*, short themes are introduced and varied in one or more of eight possible ways.
2. *Melodically oriented variations* maintain melodic content similar to that of the original theme.
3. *Harmonically oriented variations* follow the harmonic progressions of the theme.
4. *Simplified variations* eliminate notes from the original theme and maintain only the theme's general outline.
5. *Variations in the opposite mode* are those written in a major key if the original theme is in a minor key and vice versa.
6. *Double variations* are those wherein a variation serves as a theme and is thereafter varied.
7. *Contrapuntal variations* introduce new thematic material before the variation is completed, or vary the original theme using fugal devices.
8. *Character variations* manipulate the theme to take on the qualities of a recognizable genre such as a minuet, gigue, march, and so on.
9. *In free variations* any changes can be made to the theme as long as it remains remotely recognizable.

Group activities:

1. Listen to an example of a composition in sectional variation form. Identify and sing the original theme. Determine what variation types are used throughout the composition and the beginning and end of each section.

2. Select a short passage from your band folder and play it through as a class until it is memorized by each student. Select a type of sectional variation and invite a student to play the theme in that variation. (Double variations, harmonically oriented variations, and contrapuntal variations would not be appropriate for this activity.)

Name: _____

FORM
Lesson Seven—Assignment One

Part one: Identify the described variations as follows: MOV=melodically oriented; HOV=harmonically oriented; SV=simple; VOM=in the opposite mode; DV=double; CNV=canonic; CV=character; FV=free.

THEME
A fried hamburger patty.

VARIATION

____ 1. Covered with salsa, cheese, guacamole, and refried beans and stuffed in a soft tortilla shell.

____ 2. Replaced by a turkey burger patty.

____ 3. Spiced up with a little ketchup or steak sauce.

____ 4. "Make your own burger," anything goes.

____ 5. Covered with cheese, placed in a bun and topped with another patty covered with cheese *and* a pickle in a bun.

____ 6. Broken into bits and stirred in with meat substitute. (Only general "taste" remains.)

____ 7. Topped with bacon, then with turkey, then with ham…

____ 8. Remove all fat—made lean before frying.

Part two: Listen to a composition in sectional variation form. Identify two distinct portions and the type of variation used.

1.

2.

FORM

Lesson Eight

Lesson objective: To define ostinato and to introduce two types of continuous variation forms—the passacaglia and the chaconne.

Advance preparation: Have a recording of a passacaglia and a chaconne.

Concept statements:

1. The theme of a *continuous variation* is one or two phrases long and usually ends on the dominant chord (V), which serves as the beginning of the first variation. The overlapping, or "dovetail," of the theme and its variation prevents a defined cadence point and clear boundary of sections thus—*continuous variation*.

2. Continuous variation forms are of two types: *passacaglia* and *chaconne*.

3. In a passacaglia the theme functions as an *ostinato* in the bass voice. An ostinato is a continuously recurring rhythmic or melodic figure persistent throughout a composition. The theme usually remains in the bass voice though it may be ornamented and varied. The upper voices have their own rhythmic, harmonic, textural, and melodic identities.

4. The chaconne is similar to the passacaglia and the two terms are often used interchangeably. In a chaconne, however, the bass voice maintains a fixed *harmonic pattern* only; not an actual basso ostinato.

Group activities:

1. Listen to the recordings of both the passacaglia and the chaconne. Identify the themes and discuss how they are used in the compositions.

2. If possible, examine the scores of a passacaglia and chaconne to note the differences in the use of the original theme and harmonic pattern.

3. Compose a short, short theme that the students can memorize quickly. Instruct the low brass instrumentalists to play the part over and over while selected students improvise a part "above" it one at a time.

Name: _____

FORM
Lesson Eight—Assignment One

Part one: Name and describe the two types of continuous variation forms.

1.

2.

Part two: Name one band composition in continuous variation form. (Refer to your band music library, or school/public library music encyclopedias.)

FORM
Unit Quiz

Part one: Correctly label the parts of each compositional form using the words and elements from the list below. The words and elements may be used more than once or not at all.

FINAL SECTION	TWO REPRISE	FUGUE
TERNARY FORM	SONATINA	TRANSITION
BRIDGE	A	EPISODE
BAR FORM	A'	RECAPITULATION
SONATA ALLEGRO	A''	DEVELOPMENT
SIMPLE BINARY	B	CODETTA
FIRST SECTION	B'	MIDDLE ENTRY
RETRANSITION	B''	SUBORDINATE THEME
EXPOSITION	C	ROUNDED BINARY
CLOSING THEME	C'	INVERTED BAR FORM
CODA	C''	PRINCIPAL THEME
RONDO		

1.

Sop.

Alto

Tenor

Bass

Sop.

Alto

Tenor

Bass

Sop.

Alto

Tenor

Bass

©1998 by Parker Publishing Company, Inc.

2.

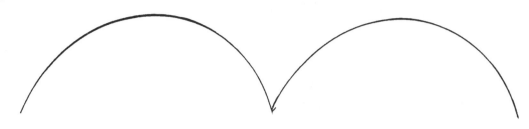

3.

4.

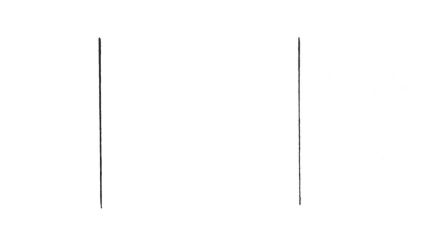

5.

FORM Unit Quiz *(cont.)*

Part two: Identify the represented fugal devices as follows: R=retrograde, I=inverted, M=mirror, S=stretto, TA=tonal answer, RA=real answer, A=augmented, D=diminished.

SUBJECT

ANSWERS

____ 1.

____ 2.

____ 3.

____ 4.

____ 5.

____ 6.

____ 7.

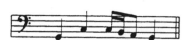

____ 8.

FORM Unit Quiz (cont.)

Part three: Arrange the terms from the list at right to fit the outline form. Then match the terms with descriptions from the list below.

___ I.

    ___ A.

        ___ 1.

        ___ 2.

        ___ 3.

        ___ 4.

        ___ 5.

        ___ 6.

        ___ 7.

        ___ 8.

    ___ B.

        ___ 1.

        ___ 2.

___ II.

CHARACTER VARIATION
SONATA ALLEGRO
SECTIONAL VARIATION
VARIATION IN OPPOSITE MODE
CANONIC VARIATION
CONTINUOUS VARIATION
MELODIC ORIENTATION VAR.
CHACONNE
FREE VARIATION
DOUBLE VARIATION
PASSACAGLIA
VARIATION FORM
HARMONIC ORIENTATION VAR.
SIMPLE VARIATION

a. maintain melody

b. variation of a variation

c. polyphonic variation

d. large, ternary form

e. no break between variations

f. continuous harmonic progression only

g. take away notes, leave only corners

h. any variation will do

i. basso ostinato

j. alter melody, keep harmony

k. theme is manipulated in this compositional form

l. variation in particular style

m. obvious break between vars.

n. e. g., d min. instead of D Maj.

ANSWER KEYS

UNIT ONE: LINEAR PITCH

Vocabulary Worksheet

Part one: Part two: Part three:

1. F   1. scale   1. b.
2. F   2. natural   2. a.
3. T   3. a.
4. T
5. T

Lesson One—Assignment One

Part one:

1. C   2. G♭   3. E♭   4. F♯   5. G♭   6. F   7. B   8. C♯   9. G   10. E

1. A   2. G♯   3. C   4. A♭   5. F   6. C   7. B♭   8. E♭   9. D♯   10. G

Part two: Part three:

1. bass   1. C   2. B   3. F   4. G♭   5. C

2. treble   1. G♯   2. C   3. G♯   4. G♭   5. C♯

3. Interval

4. ledger

5. sharp

Lesson Two—Assignment One

Part one:

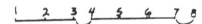

Part two:

Tonic note

1. C

2. F

3. B♭

4. E♭

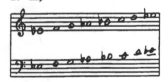

5. A♭

6. D♭

Lesson Three—Assignment One

Part one:

Part two:

Part three:

1. B♭

2. A

3. D

4. D♭

5. F

6. E♭

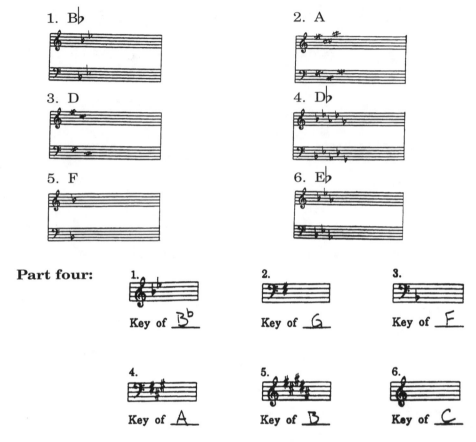

Part four:

1. Key of B♭
2. Key of G
3. Key of F
4. Key of A
5. Key of B
6. Key of C

Part five: Answers will vary

Lesson Four—Assignment One

Part one:

1. A♭

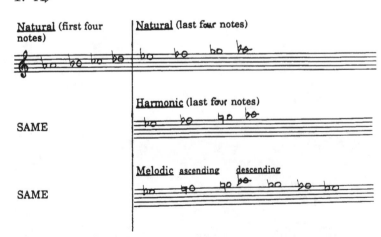

Natural (first four notes)

Natural (last four notes)

SAME   Harmonic (last four notes)

SAME   Melodic ascending   descending

2. F

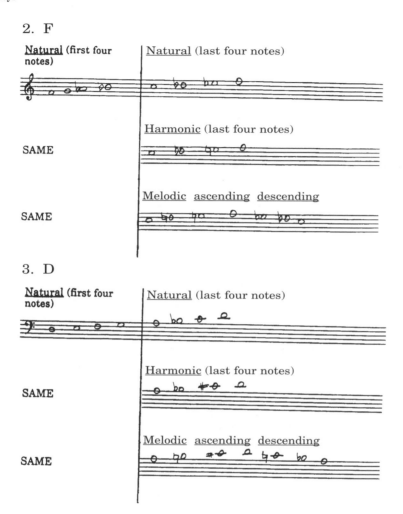

| Natural (first four notes) | Natural (last four notes) |

SAME | Harmonic (last four notes) |

SAME | Melodic ascending descending |

3. D

| Natural (first four notes) | Natural (last four notes) |

SAME | Harmonic (last four notes) |

SAME | Melodic ascending descending |

Part two: Answers will vary

Part three: Answers will vary

Part four: Answers will vary

Lesson Five—Assignment One

Part one:

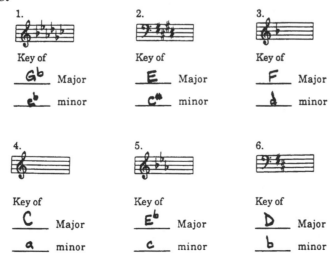

1.
Key of
_Gb_ Major
_eb_ minor

2.
Key of
_E_ Major
_c#_ minor

3.
Key of
_F_ Major
_d_ minor

4.
Key of
_C_ Major
_a_ minor

5.
Key of
_Eb_ Major
_c_ minor

6.
Key of
_D_ Major
_b_ minor

Part two:

1.
Major:
E♭ F G A♭ B♭ C D E♭
minor:

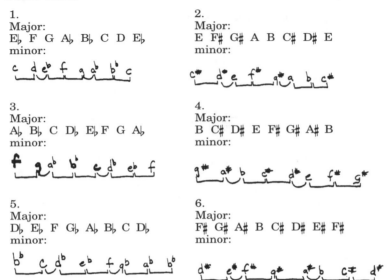

2.
Major:
E F♯ G♯ A B C♯ D♯ E
minor:

3.
Major:
A♭ B♭ C D♭ E♭ F G A♭
minor:

4.
Major:
B C♯ D♯ E F♯ G♯ A♯ B
minor:

5.
Major:
D♭ E♭ F G♭ A♭ B♭ C D♭
minor:

6.
Major:
F♯ G♯ A♯ B C♯ D♯ E♯ F♯
minor:

Part three: Answers will vary

Lesson Six—Assignment One

Part one:

1. 3   2. 8   3. 5   4. 5   5. 6   6. 6   7. 6   8. 4   9. 2   10. 3

11. 3   12. 5   13. 2   14. 6   15. 4   16. 8   17. 6   18. 4   19. 2   20. 5

Part two:

1. ↑5   2. ↓3   3. ↑4   4. ↓7   5. ↓6   6. ↑2

Part three:

A
1. ↓5
D

G
2. ↓3
E

F
3. ↑4
C

C
4. ↑2
B

D
5. ↓7
E

B
6. ↑6
D

Part four:

1. diminished, minor, major, perfect, augmented
2. letter
3. semi-tones
4. 3, 5, 4, 2

Lesson Seven—Assignment One

Part one:

___ ___ ___ P8 P4 P5 ___ P4 ___ P5 P4 ___ ___

Part two:

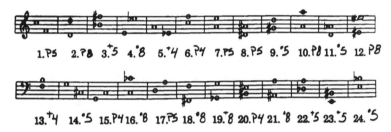

1.P5 2.P8 3.⁺5 4.°8 5.⁺4 6.P4 7.P5 8.P5 9.°5 10.P8 11.°5 12.P8

13.⁺4 14.°5 15.P4 16.°8 17.P5 18.°8 19.°8 20.P4 21.°8 22.°5 23.°5 24.°5

Part three: Answers will vary

Part four: 1. e, 2. c, 3. a

Lesson Eight—Assignment One

Part one:

A.	°2	m2	M2	+2
	1. ↓	2. ↓	3. ↓	4. ↑
	5. ↓	6. ↑	7. ↓	8. ↓
	9. ↑	10. ↓	11. ↑	12. ↓
	13. ↑	14. ↓	15. ↑	16. ↓

B.

| °3 | m3 | M3 | +3 |

1. ↑   2. ↑   3. ↓   4. ↓

5. ↓   6. ↑   7. ↑   8. ↓

9. ↑   10. ↓   11. ↑   12. ↓

13. ↑   14. ↑   15. ↓   16. ↓

C.

| °6 | m6 | M6 | +6 |

1. ↑   2. ↑   3. ↓   4. ↑

D.

| °7 | m7 | M7 | +7 |

1. ↓   2. ↑   3. ↓   4. ↑

5. ↑   6. ↓   7. ↑   8. ↑

Part two:

1. m3   2. m3   3. °2   4. P8   5. +5   6. P4   7. P5   8. m6   9. m7   10. +5

Lesson Nine—Assignment One

Part one:

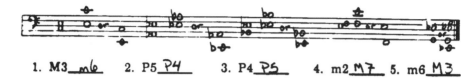

1. M3 _m6_   2. P5 _P4_   3. P4 _P5_   4. m2 _M7_   5. m6 _M3_

Part two:

1. P4 _P5_   2. °5 _+4_   3. +5 _°4_   4. m6 _M3_   5. M7 _m2_

6. °6 _+3_   7. M2 _m7_   8. m3 _M6_   9. P4 _P5_   10. +2 _°7_

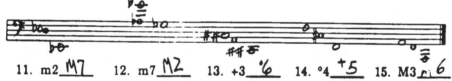

11. m2 _M7_   12. m7 _M2_   13. +3 _°6_   14. °4 _+5_   15. M3 _m6_

Part three:

1. Strict

2. Tonal

Part four: Answers will vary

Lesson Ten—Assignment One

Part one: Answers will vary

Part two: Answers will vary

LINEAR PITCH UNIT QUIZ

Part one:

Part two:

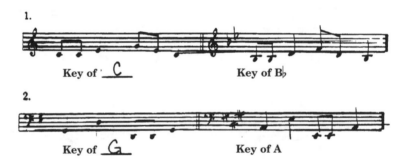

Part three:

1. (Accidentals)

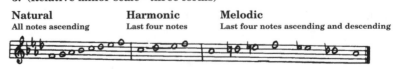

2. (Using key signature)

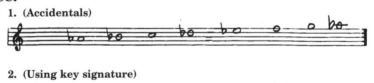

3. (Relative minor scale—three forms)

Natural
All notes ascending

Harmonic
Last four notes

Melodic
Last four notes ascending and descending

Part four:

1. D Major

2. a minor

3. g minor

4. E Major

5. B Major

6. D♭ Major

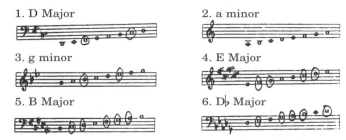

Part five:

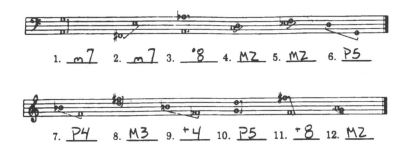

1. m7   2. m7   3. °8   4. M2   5. M2   6. P5

7. P4   8. M3   9. +4   10. P5   11. +8   12. M2

Part six:

1. P5 P4   2. M3 m6   3. m3 M6   4. m2 M7

5. P5 P4   6. M3 m6   7. M7 m2   8. m2 M7

Part seven:

UNIT TWO: VERTICAL PITCH

Vocabulary Worksheet

Part one:

1. T	5. F
2. T	6. F
3. T	7. T
4. T	8. F

Part two:

1. counterpoint
2. mezzo soprano

Part three:

1. a.
2. b.

Lesson One—Assignment One

Part one:

1. triad
2. thirds
3. fifth
4. arpeggio
5. perfect

Part two:

Part three:

Lesson Two—Assignment One

Part one:

Part two:

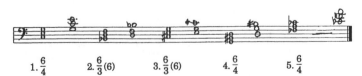

Part three:

1. e   6. b
2. d   7. f
3. c   8. i
4. a   9. h
5. g

Lesson Three—Assignment One

Part one:

Part two: Answers will vary

Part three: Answers will vary

Part four:

Lesson Four—Assignment One

Part one:

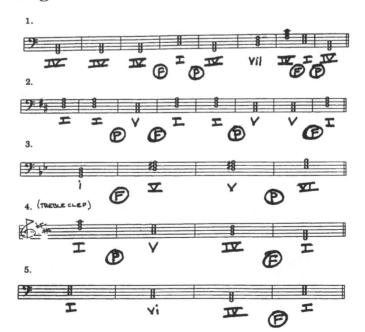

Part two:

1.

2.

Schumann

3.

Grieg

4.

Chopin

5.

Mozart

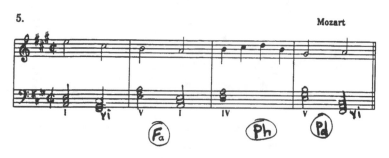

6.

7.

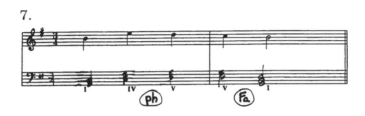

8.

VERTICAL PITCH UNIT QUIZ

Part one:

1. b	6. e
2. i	7. d
3. g	8. h
4. c	9. f
5. a	

Part two:

1. R 2. $\frac{6}{3}$ 3. $\frac{6}{4}$ 4. $\frac{6}{4}$ 5. $\frac{6}{3}$

6. R 7. $\frac{6}{3}$ 8. $\frac{6}{3}$ 9. $\frac{6}{4}$ 10. $\frac{6}{3}$

Part three:

Part four: Answers will vary on all examples

UNIT THREE: DURATION

Vocabulary Worksheet

Part one: **Part two:**   **Part three:**

1. T   1. tempo   6. tie   1. a.
2. T   2. bar line   7. beat   2. a.
3. T   3. rhythm   8. meter/time signature
4. F   4. upbeat   9. syncopation
5. T   5. dot   10. subdividing

Lesson One—Assignment One

Part one:

1. Mary had a little lamb, little lamb, little lamb.

| > ∪ >∪ | >∪ >∪ | > ∪ > ∪ | >∪ >∪ |

2. Blueberry, apple and pumpkin pie too.

>∪∪ | >∪∪ | > ∪∪ | >∪∪

Part two:

1. Triple meter—three pulses per measure.

| > ∪∪ |

2. Duple meter—two pulses per measure.

| > ∪ |

3. Quadruple meter—four pulses per measure.

| > ∪>∪ |

4. Quintuple meter—five pulses per measure (arranged in twos and threes, or threes and twos).

|>∪∪ >∪ | or |>∪ >∪∪ |

Part three:

1. "Yankee Doodle"   3. "Oh Susannah"

Meter $\frac{2}{4}$ Meter $\frac{4}{4}$

Accent pattern > ∪   Accent pattern >∪> ∪

2. "America the Beautiful"   4. "Old McDonald Had a Farm"

Meter $\frac{4}{4}$ Meter $\frac{2}{4}$

Accent pattern > ∪>∪   Accent pattern > ∪

Part four: Answers will vary

Lesson Two—Assignment One

Part one:

1. r	11. f
2. g	12. c
3. d	13. i
4. m	14. s
5. a	15. o
6. b	16. j
7. e	17. p
8. k	18. h
9. h	19. q
10. t	20. l

Part two:

1. 4
2. 2
3. ○ (whole note)
4. 3
5. ♩. (dotted quarter note)

Part three:

Lesson Three—Assignment One

Part one:

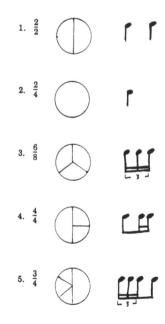

Part two:

1. $\frac{3}{4}$

2. $\frac{2}{2}$

3. $\frac{3}{4}$

4. $\frac{6}{8}$

5. $\frac{2}{4}$

Part three:

1. $\frac{4}{4}$ 1 e + da

2. $\frac{2}{2}$ 1 e + da

3. $\frac{4}{4}$ 1 - + -

4. $\frac{4}{4}$ 1 - + da

5. $\frac{2}{2}$ 1 e + -

Lesson Three—Assignment Two

Part one: Answers will vary

Part two: Answers will vary

Lesson Four—Assignment One

Part one:

1. dot

2. tie

3. tie

4. dot

5. dot

6. tie

7. dot

8. tie

9. tie

10. tie

Part two:

1. A   2. R   3. R   4. A

Part three: Answers will vary

Lesson Five—Assignment One

Part one:

C 1.
X 2.
C 3.
S 4.
X 5.

S 6.
S 7.
X 8.
C 9.
S 10.

Part two:

1.
2.
3.
4.

Part three:

X 1.
X 2.
S 3.
X 4.
X 5.

S 6.
X 7.
C 8.
X 9.
C 10.

Lesson Six—Assignment One

Part one:

1.

2.

3.

4.

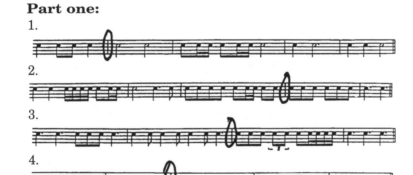

Part two:

DURATION UNIT QUIZ

Part one:

1.   5.

2.   6.

3.   7.

4.   8.

Part two:

S 1.   C 6.

S 2.   S 7.

S 3.   X 8.

C 4.   S 9.

C 5.   X 10.

Part three:

1.   6.

2.   7.

3.   8.

4.   9.

5.   10.

Part four:

1.

2.

3.

4.

5.

Part five:

1. Pulse to pulse

   [♩ = ♩]

   3/4 to 3/2

2. Division to division

   [♪ = ♪]

   4/4 to 12/8

3. No change in pulse note value

   [♩ = ♩]

   3/4 to 4/4

4. Pulse to division

   [♪ = ♪]

   4/8 to 4/4

5. Division to pulse

   [♪ = ♩]

   7/8 to 3/4

UNIT FOUR: ACOUSTICS

Vocabulary Worksheet

Part one:

1. F	6. T
2. F	7. T
3. F	8. T
4. T	9. T
5. T	10. T

Part two:

1. beats
2. acoustics
3. transposing
4. melodic
5. slide

Part three:

1. b.
2. c.
3. b.
4. b.

Lesson One—Assignment One

Part one:

A. timbre-harmonics-overtone
B. frequency-pitch
C. amplitude-volume-intensity

Part two:

1. H	6. L
2. F	7. T
3. L	8. T
4. T	9. H
5. H	10. F

Lesson Two—Assignment One

Part one:

BRASS	WOODWINDS	STRINGS
trumpet	tenor saxophone	cello
baritone	bassoon	piano
trombone	flute	harpsichord
tuba	oboe	viola
French horn	soprano saxophone	
	alto flute	
	English horn	

PITCHED PERCUSSION	NON-PITCHED PERCUSSION
chimes	snare drum
timpani	suspended cymbal
	tambourine

Part two: Answers will vary

Part three: Answers will vary

Lesson Three—Assignment One

Part one:

1.   2.   3.   4.

5.   6.   7.   8.

Lesson Four—Assignment One

Part one:

Trumpet:			F Horn:			Tuba:		
II	≤	I	III	≥	I	I+III	≥	II
III	=	I+II	I	≤	III+II	I+II+III	≥	III
I+III	≥	I+II	II	≤	III	Open	≤	I

Part two:

T Saxophone   T Tuba   N Oboe   N Flute   N Bassoon

N Trombone   T Clarinet   T Trumpet   T F Horn

Part three:

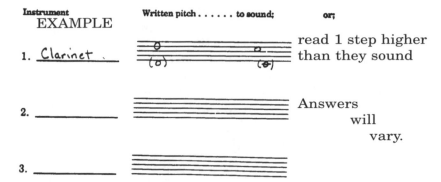

Instrument	Written pitch . . . . . . to sound;	or;
EXAMPLE		
1. Clarinet		read 1 step higher than they sound
2. _____		Answers will vary.
3. _____		

Part four:

TUBA

Co.	O	V
PT.	NT	

TRUMPET

Cy.	O	V
NPT	T	

FLUTE

Cy.	O	SH
PT	NT	

CLARINET

Cy.	C	SH
PT	T	

F HORN

Co.	O	V
NPT	T	

SAXOPHONE

Co.	O	SH
PT	T	

BASSOON

Co.	O	SH
PT	NT	

TROMBONE

Cy.	O	S
NPT	NT	

Lesson Five—Assignment One

Part one:
Example: arch the tongue
Answers will vary

Part two:
Example: insufficient air support
Answers will vary

Part three:
Example: 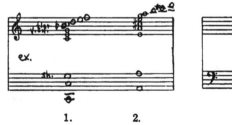 on trumpet I + III, use III valve slide
Answers will vary

ACOUSTICS UNIT QUIZ

Part one:

1. A	6. D
2. B	7. B
3. D	8. B
4. A	9. A
5. C	10. D

Part two:

1. cents	6. transposing
2. conical	7. fundamental
3. tongue	8. beats
4. overtones	9. alternate
5. timbre	10. rise

Part three:

Answers will vary

UNIT FIVE: STYLE

Vocabulary Worksheet

Part one:

1. F
2. F
3. T
4. T
5. T

Part two:

1. aleatory
2. alberti bass
3. Antiphony
4. Chant
5. jazz

6. lyrical
7. scherzo
8. program music
9. melismatic
10. leitmotif

Part three:

1. c.
2. c.

Lesson One—Assignment One

Part one:

1. Answers will vary
2. Answers will vary

Part two:

1. EE
2. CU
3. EE
4. EE
5. CU

6. CU
7. EE
8. EE
9. EE
10. CU

Answers to the second part of this exercise will vary.

Lesson Two—Assignment One

Part one:

1. g
2. b
3. a
4. e
5. c

6. i
7. j
8. h
9. f
10. d

Part two:
   C O P

Part three: Answers will vary

Lesson Three—Assignment One

Part one:

1. 1450 to 1600
2. Columbus discovered America
   Michelangelo created his frescoes in the Sistine Chapel in the
      Vatican at Rome
   Cortez conquered Mexico
   Gutenberg invented movable type
3. rebirth and secular (Answers will vary)
4. growth and chromatic (Answers will vary)
5. fugue and suite (madrigal, aria, chanson, chorale, canzona, toccata)

Part two: Answers will vary

Part three: Answers will vary

Lesson Four—Assignment One

Part one:

1. 1600 to 1750
2. Mayflower, Bay Psalm Book, Peter the Great
3. Shakespeare, Milton, Rembrandt, Descartes, Newton, Bacon, Galileo
4. basso continuo, extreme contrasts, specific mediums, music classified, metric patterns
5. oratorio, passacaglia, opera, chaconne, suite

Part two: Answers will vary

Part three: Answers will vary

Lesson Five—Assignment One

Part one:

1. 1750 to 1825
2. metronome, steam engine, French and American revolutions
3. individual, equality
4. alberti bass, established phrases, gradual dynamic changes, contrast within theme
5. sonata, symphony

Part two: Answers will vary

Part three: Answers will vary

Lesson Six—Assignment One

Part one:

1. 1825 to 1900
2. theory of evolution, electricity, phonograph, telegraph, Lincoln assassinated
3. seize eternity, literary expression
4. impressionism, realism
5. lyrical, chromatic, extreme

Part two: Answers will vary

Part three: Answers will vary

Lesson Seven—Assignment One

Part one:

1. romantic
2. transportation advances, communication advances, wars, equal rights
3. satellite, compact discs
4. serial music
5. aleatory

Part two: Answers will vary

Part three: Answers will vary

Lesson Seven—Assignment Two

Part one: Answers will vary

Part two: Answers will vary

STYLE UNIT QUIZ

Part one:

	time frame	music period	hist. setting	philos. infl.	music char.	forms intro.	infl. comp.
1.	q	aa	t	g tt	v	n	p
2.	h	l	a	w	bb pp	uu	kk dd
3.	w	mm	ff	d	y	r	i
4.	hh	e	rr	b	o	cc	j
5.	c	s	ee	gg	u	ss	m x jj
6.	qq	z	ii	oo	k	f	ll

Part two: Answers will vary

Part three: Answers will vary

UNIT SIX: FORM

Vocabulary Worksheet

Part one:
1. T
2. T
3. F
4. F
5. T

Part two:
1. exposition
2. real answer
3. augmentation
4. dependent
5. trio

Part three:
1. b.
2. c.
3. b.

Lesson One—Assignment One

Part one:

Part two: Answers will vary

Lesson Two—Assignment One

Part one:

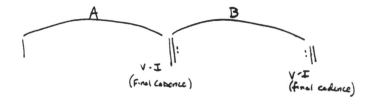

Part two:
—ROUNDED BINARY needs a return of "A" material in the B section.
—BAR FORM is a repeat of "A" section **ONLY**.
—TWO REPRISE is a repeat of "A" section **AND** "B" section.

Lesson Three—Assignment One

Part one:

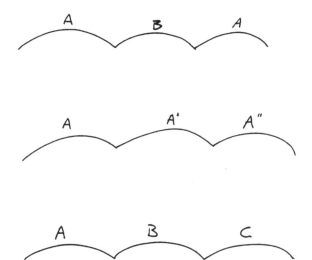

Lesson Four—Assignment One

Part one:

First Section		Middle Entry		Final Section	
exposition	episode	exposition	episode		
1. answer[1]	fragments			1	all voices
2. subject	of			2	in until
3. answer[2]	subject	subject		3	the end.
4. answer[3]	modulation	answer		4	

New Key

Part two:
1. Mirror   (retrograde)
2. Augmentation   (stretto)
3. Diminution

Part three: Answers will vary

Lesson Five—Assignment One

Part one:

Exposition	**Development**	**Recapitulation**
P.T. trans. S.T. C.T.	retrans.	P.T. trans. S.T. C.T. (coda)
I I -------- v -------- v	v --------------------!------ v	I I I -------- I

Part two:
No development section. The middle part is replaced by a short "bridge." (A bridge joins sections, whereas a transition joins themes.)

Lesson Six—Assignment One

Part one:

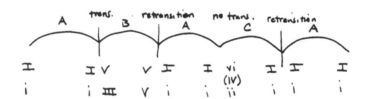

Part two: Answers will vary

Lesson Seven—Assignment One

Part one:
1. CV
2. VOM
3. SV
4. FV
5. DV
6. HOV
7. CNV
8. MOV

Part two: Answers will vary

Lesson Eight—Assignment One

Part one:
1. Passacaglia—uses basso ostinato throughout piece as a "ground" for everything else.
2. Chaconne—like passacaglia except only a harmonic pattern continues; without sense of repeated theme in the bass.

Part two: Answers will vary

FORM UNIT QUIZ

Part one:

1. FUGUE   First Section

Sop.

Alto   exposition   ┆   episode

Tenor

Bass

                                                Middle Entry

Sop.

Alto   exposition   ┆   episode

Tenor

Bass

                                                Final Section

Sop.

Alto

Tenor

Bass

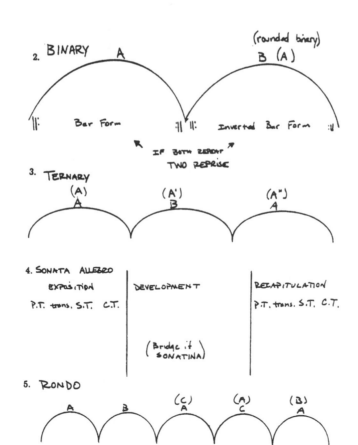

230

Answer Keys

Part two:
1. M
2. S
3. RA
4. I
5. A
6. R
7. D
8. TA

Part three:

<u>k</u> I. VARIATION FORM   CHARACTER VARIATION

      <u>m</u> A. SECTIONAL VARIATION   SONATA ALLEGRO

                <u>j</u> 1. MOV   SECTIONAL VARIATION

                <u>q</u> 2. HOV   VARIATION IN OPPOSITE MODE

These may be listed in different order   <u>c</u> 3. CNV   CANONIC VARIATION

                <u>l</u> 4. CV   CONTINUOUS VARIATION

                <u>h</u> 5. FV   MELODIC ORIENTATION VAR.

                <u>a</u> 6. SV   CHACONNE

                <u>b</u> 7. DV   FREE VARIATION

                <u>n</u> 8. VOM   DOUBLE VARIATION

      <u>e</u> B. CONTINUOUS VARIATION   PASSACAGLIA

                <u>i</u> 1. PASSACAGLIA   VARIATION FORM

                <u>f</u> 2. CHACONNE   HARMONIC ORIENTATION VAR.

    <u>d</u> II. SONATA ALLEGRO   SIMPLE VARIATION

a. maintain melody
b. variation of a variation
c. polyphonic variation
d. large, ternary form
e. no break between variations
f. continuous harmonic progression only
g. take away notes, leave only corners

h. any variation will do
i. basso ostinato
j. alter melody, keep harmony
k. theme is manipulated in this compositional form
l. variation in particular style
m. obvious break between vars.
n. e.g., d min. instead of D Maj.

APPENDICES

Appendix 1

GAMES AND ACTIVITIES

Music Notation

Activity objective: To present the concept of notation in a novel and entertaining way.

Advance preparation: Make transparencies of the accompanying symbols and notation pages. Have an overhead projector and screen set up for use in class.

Activity instructions:

1. Read or paraphrase the following story:

    Once upon a time the earth was inhabited by beast-hunting cavemen who had only primitive forms of communication and **no** cultural activity. One particular cave family consisted of papa cave—we'll call him "Ug," mama cave—"Katug," and toddler cave—"Thug." One day, after chasing a dinosaur all around the big volcano, Ug stopped to rest and happened to lean his head on his hand—fingers just under the jaw bone and on his neck below the ear. He felt a strange pounding sensation against his finger and began to nod his head with each throb. Eventually, the pounding diminished to a steady, but soft "thump, thump, thump," and Ug's nods slowed. Ug was so excited about his new discovery that he raced home to tell Katug. Bursting into the cave, Ug found Katug hurriedly plucking the large pterodactyl he had brought home the day before. Ug grabbed for Katug's hand and placed her fingers on his neck, just where his fingers had been earlier that day. Katug looked startled but soon began nodding with the throbs. Just as before, the pounding slowed and softened until it was a steady "thump, thump, thump." In their excitement, Ug and Katug named the experience "bug," and went about sharing their discovery with the entire cave village—never imagining the impact of their find on future generations in the form of what we know as *pulse, beat, tempo, accelerando,* and *retardando.*

    Several cave years passed and literally the whole village was bouncing, nodding, and dancing to the beat of their resting and laboring heartrates. At some point, the village chiefs decided to organize the unending pulses into groups and since counting had only been developed to the number four (cave people had only four fingers and no thumb), continuous pulses were counted "rug, snug, pug, mug," over and over again.

    At some point in the history, Ug set out on the most dangerous adventure of a caveman's life—to hunt the sabre-toothed tiger. Ug had stalked the

232

creature several weeks earlier and knew of the tiger's den not far from the village. Ug was gone only a few days when Katug decided to take him some lunch. Little did she know that trailing behind her was little Thug, anxious for an adventure and carrying along his diary. (He never went anywhere without it.)

After a long hike, Katug came to the scene of action—a blur of sight and sound as the tiger and Ug raced 'round and 'round in the small clearing. First the tiger ran by, giving a huge growl at each lap. And close behind was Ug waving his club and giving a snort as he passed by Katug. Over and over the sound—GROWL UGH, GROWL UGH. Then, suddenly, the tiger caught the scent of Katug and reeled to face her just as little Thug came through the underbrush. Thug was just in time to hear his mother's shriek and see the race begin anew; father, mother, and the ferocious tiger running madly around the clearing—SHRIEK GROWL UGH, SHRIEK GROWL UGH; then UGH UGH GROWL SHRIEK, and GROWL GROWL UGH SHRIEK. Thug knew he was helpless; he could only hide and watch the terrible scene. Gaining some presence of mind, however, Thug realized he *could* record the event for future generations. He pulled out his diary, took a check of his speeding heartrate—"rug, snug, pug, mug; rug, snug, pug, mug" and began to write. For each pulse with a shriek, he drew a mark like this: !. For each pulse with a growl, he drew a mark like this: *. For each pulse with an ugh, he drew a mark like this: >. For each pulse that passed with no sound, Thug drew no symbol and when a sound extended from one pulse to another, he drew a -.

The tiger hunt had quite an unhappy ending, a terrible thing for even a cave boy to witness. But the bright part of the story is the record Thug made and its impact on the development of musical notation as we know it today. We have a page of Thug's diary and are going to read through it as a class.

2. Project the transparency of symbols onto the screen. Divide the class into three groups and assign group one to sound a "shriek" on each pulse that is written !. Assign group two to sound a "growl" on each pulse that is written *. Assign group three to sound an "ugh" on each pulse that is written >.

3. After reading through the symbol sheet, and trading parts as desired, explain that eventually the symbols became too cumbersome for the broadening vocabulary of sounds. Alphabets were developed for writing out the words of a story and notation was developed to represent sounds of pitches and rhythms.

4. Project the notation transparency on the screen. Demonstrate the relationship of the two transparencies (the "shriek" symbol is replaced by the written note F, the "growl" symbol is replaced by the written note B, and the "ugh" is replaced by the written note E—rhythms are familiar eighths, quarters and halves) and read through the "diary page" again.

Thug's Diary—original

```
1.  |   |   |   |   |   |   |   |   |   |   |   |   |   |   |
    *   *   !   -   >   !   !   *   >   -   -   *   !   !   >   *


2.  |   |   |   |   |   |   |   |   |   |   |   |   |   |   |
    !   !   !   -   >> >>  *   -   !!  >>  !!  >>  *       *   >


3.  |   |   |   |   |   |   |   |   |   |   |   |   |   |   |
    *   -   -   >   !>  !>  ** *   >>  !   ** >   !   -   -   >


4.  |   |   |   |   |   |   |   |   |   |   |   |   |   |   |
    >   -   *   -   >   -   *   -   !!!! >   ** >   *


5.  |   |   |   |   |   |   |   |   |   |   |   |   |   |   |
    *       >       *       !         ** >>  !!  !   >>>> !!  *   -


6.  |   |   |   |   |   |   |   |   |   |   |   |   |   |   |
    *   *   *   *   !!  >>          *   *   *   *   !!  >>  *   -


7.  |   |   |   |   |   |   |   |   |   |   |   |   |   |   |
    !   -   -   -   -   -   -   >   ****    >>      *>  *>  !!  >


8.  |   |   |   |   |   |   |   |   |   |   |   |   |   |   |
    !>  *>  !>  *>  !!  >>  ** >>  !!!! >   >   >   *   *   >!  *
```

234

Thug's Diary—transcribed

Name: _____

MUSIC NOTATION—ASSIGNMENT

Part one: Under each line, replace the symbols with modern notation (rhythms only, not pitches). Above each line, write in the counting.

1. | | | | | | | | | | | | | | | |
    ! ! ! - >> >> * - !! >> !! >> *   * >

2. | | | | | | | | | | | | | | | |
    * - - > !> !> ** * >> ! ** > ! - - >

3. | | | | | | | | | | | | | | | |
    > - * - > - * - !!!! > ** > *

4. | | | | | | | | | | | | | | | | |
    *   >   *   !   ** >> !! ! >>>> !!   * -

5. | | | | | | | | | | | | | | | |
    * * * * !! >>   * * * * !! >> * -

6. | | | | | | | | | | | | | | | |
    ! - - - - - - > **** >>   *> *> !! >

7. | | | | | | | | | | | | | | | |
    !> *> !> *> !! >> ** >> !!!! > > > * * >! *

236

APPENDIX 1, Music Notation—Assignment *(cont.)*

Part two: Compose an eight-measure piece using symbols of your choice to represent sounds or pitches. Carefully organize the symbol groupings to represent rhythms. Provide a LEGEND to define the symbols you choose.

Music Notation—Assignment Answer Key

Part one:

Part two: Answers will vary

Major Scales and Intervals

Game objective: To provide the students with practice in writing and singing major scales and identifying intervals while competing as teams in class. The game involves three levels of challenge and points are awarded at each level. The overall team objective is to gain more points than the other teams.

Advance preparation: Make a large poster showing at least one octave of a piano keyboard. Label each key with its letter name(s): e. g., A♭/G♯, C♯/D♭. (Butcher paper is recommended and total length should be about six feet.) Hang the poster on the chalkboard or wall and tape a line on the floor about five yards in front of the poster. Each student needs a page of staff paper and pencil. The third stage of play requires a toy dart gun and a prize should be prepared for the winning team.

Concept statements:
1. Each scale follows a set pattern of whole-steps and half-steps.
2. Major scales starting on some pitches require sharps and flats to maintain the scale pattern.

Game instructions:
1. Divide the class into three teams, designate a team captain for each and instruct each team to sit in a circle.

Level One

2. Name a pitch and instruct all students to write the notes of the major scale beginning on the pitch named. Each pitch should be written with accidentals as required to form the proper whole-step, half-step pattern. DO NOT USE KEY SIGNATURES. (It may be necessary to give hints, for example, "This scale requires three sharps.")

3. Instruct the students to work alone for the first two minutes and then allow team members to help those who are not finished.

4. As each member of a team finishes, he should lay his pencil on the floor. When an entire team is finished, the team captain should raise his hand. Note the order in which teams finish.

5. Randomly select and check three papers from the first team. If all three are correct, award the team 5 points and move on to level two. If any one of the papers is incorrect, select and check three papers from the team that finished second, and so on, until you find three correct papers from one team. (Sometimes it will take two or three laps. Do not point out the specific mistakes, but allow students to correct papers you have looked at and prepare for the second time around.)

Level Two

6. Only the "winning team" of *level one* participates in this stage of the game. To gain 5 points, one student from the team must correctly sing the written scale up and down. If no student is willing to sing alone, the team can sing the scale together but gain only 3 points. After singing the scale, the team selects an individual to move to *level three*.

Level Three

7. Ask the student to name the __ step of the scale. If the student names the correct pitch, award the team 3 points. Instruct the student to step behind the taped line on the floor, face the keyboard poster, and try to shoot the correct pitch with the dart gun for 2 points.

8. At this level, a team could gain 5 points for naming the correct pitch *and* hitting it with the dart; 3 points for naming the correct pitch, but not hitting it; or 2 points for hitting the pitch after *you* have named it.

9. There are 15 points possible in each round of play. After playing all three levels, select a new scale and begin a new round.

Keys and Key Signatures

Activity objectives: (1) To present three ways of naming tones and provide experience working with them. (2) To provide simple transposing exercises and reinforce the concept of tonality within any key.

Advance preparation: Replica of piano keyboard. Piano to be used in demonstration. Notes, letter names, scale degree numbers, and solfege letters (movable "do" system) for the first eight measures of "Are You Sleeping" and "Mary had a Little Lamb" written on the chalkboard or large chart. (See the examples.) Several lines of music staff on chalkboard. Copies of the worksheet accompanying this activity.

"Are You Sleeping"

"Mary Had a Little Lamb"

Concept statements:

1. As is demonstrated with the two examples provided, there are three common ways of identifying tones: letter names A - G and inclusive sharps and flats; "Solfege" syllables—Do Re Mi Fa Sol La Ti Do; and scale degree numbers 1 - 8 (numbering the degrees does not allow for the use of accidentals).

2. Music can be written in any key by using different pitches as "tonic," following the same intervalic pattern but using different tones.

Activity instructions:

1. Have class sing through various major scales using numbers, letter names, and syllables.

2. Write various scales on the board using the different systems of note identification.

3. Select four students to participate in the activity.

Student #1 Sit at piano and "pick out" the pitches to "Are You Sleeping" *beginning on B♭.*

Student #2 At the chalkboard, write the notes to "Are You Sleeping" as student #1 plays them (start with B♭ and use accidentals to identify flats). The class should be involved in determining when the piece is written correctly.

Student #3 Replace the accidentals with the appropriate key signature.

Student #4 Identify the notes of the transposed piece with numbers and solfege syllables.

4. Follow instructions for step #3, except use the tune "Mary Had a Little Lamb" and have **student #1** "pick out" the notes on his instrument, beginning on concert G.

5. Extend the activity by using tunes or tune segments such as "Jingle Bells," "Caissons," and so on. Begin each tune on a different pitch and have students use instruments or piano to identify pitches. After tunes are written, have the class sing the tunes or play them together. (Playing tunes will require an explanation of transposing instruments and their relationship to concert, or written pitch.)

Name: _____

KEYS AND KEY SIGNATURE—ASSIGNMENT

Part one: For each of the following tunes, an example is given in one key, and written both note for note (using accidentals) and with a key signature. The three possible note names have also been included. For each example, first determine the original key, then rewrite the tune starting on the pitch as indicated and fill in the blanks with the missing information.

EXAMPLE

1. "Twinkle, Twinkle Little Star"

NOTE FOR NOTE   USING KEY SIGNATURE

Letters: B♭ B♭ F F G G F E♭ E♭ D D C C B♭   Key of

Num.   1 1 5 5 6 6 5 4   4 3 3 2 2 1   _____

Solfege: D D S S L L S F   F M M R R D

Start on C:

NOTE FOR NOTE   USING KEY SIGNATURE

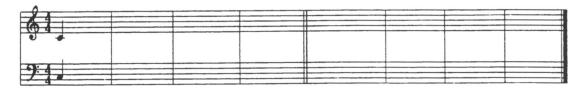

Letters: C C G G A _ _ _ F _ _ _ _ C   Key of

Num.   1 1 5 5 _ 6 5 4 4 3 _ _ 2 _   _____

Solfege: D D S S _ L _ _ _ _ M _ _ _

APPENDIX 1, Keys and Key Signature—Assignment *(cont.)*

"Twinkle. . ." cont.

Start on E♭

NOTE FOR NOTE   USING KEY SIGNATURE

Letters: E♭ E♭ B♭ B♭ _ _ _ _ _ _ _ F F E♭   Key of

Num: _ _ _ _ _ 6 _ _ 4 _ 3 _ _ 1   _____

Solfege: D D S S L L S _ _ _ _ _ _ _

EXAMPLE
2. "Row, Row, Row your Boat"

NOTE FOR NOTE

Letters: E♭ E♭ E♭ F G G F G A♭ B♭ E♭ B♭ G E♭ B♭ A♭ G F E♭
Num: 1 1 1 2 3 3 2 3 4 5 1 5 3 1 5 4 3 2 1
Solfege: D D D R M M R M F S D S M D S F M R D

USING KEY SIGNATURE

Key of _____

APPENDIX 1, Keys and Key Signature—Assignment *(cont.)*

Start on D, use a key signature or write note for note.

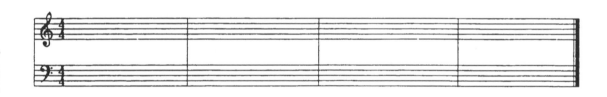

Letters: D D D E _   _ _ _ _ _   _   _ _   _   _ _ _ _

Num: 1 _ _ _ 3   _ 2 _ _ _   1   _ 3   _   _ 4 _ 2 1

Solfege: D _ _ _ _   M _ _ _   S   D   _ _   D   _ F _ _ D

Key of _____

Start on A, use a key signature or write note for note.

Letters: _____

Num. _____

Solfege: _____

Key of _____

APPENDIX 1, Keys and Key Signature—Assignment *(cont.)*

Part two: Write the last four measures of "Up on the Housetop." Start from the note indicated and fill in the blanks with all missing information.
Start on A♭, use a key signature or write note for note.

Letters: A♭ _ _ _   _ _ _   _ _ _ _ _ _   _ _ _

Num: 5 _ _ _ 3   _ 5 _   5 _ _ _ 3 _   2 _ _

Solfege: S _ _ _ _   F _ _   S _ _ _ _ M   R _ _

Key of _____

Part three: (The director should fill in the blanks before assigning this section.)
Start at letter/number _____ in our band piece _____, and rewrite _____ measures of your part beginning on the pitch one whole-step higher.

Keys and Key Signature Answer Key

Part one:

EXAMPLE
1. "Twinkle, Twinkle Little Star"
NOTE FOR NOTE   USING KEY SIGNATURE

Letters: Bb Bb F F G G F Eb Eb D D C C Bb
Num.   1 1 5 5 6 6 5 4 4 3 3 2 2 1
Solfege: D D S S L L S F F M M R R D

Key of
Bb

Start on C:
NOTE FOR NOTE   USING KEY SIGNATURE

Letters: C C G G A A G E F E E D D C
Num.   1 1 5 5 6 6 5 4 4 3 3 2 2 1
Solfege: D D S S L L S F F M M R R D

Key of
C

Start on Eb
NOTE FOR NOTE   USING KEY SIGNATURE

Letters: Eb Eb Bb Bb C C Bb A A G G F F Eb
Num.   1 1 5 5 6 6 5 4 4 3 3 2 2 1
Solfege: D D S S L L S F F M M R R D

Key of
Eb

EXAMPLE
2. "Row, Row, Row your Boat"
NOTE FOR NOTE

Letters: Eb Eb Eb F G   G F G A Bb   Eb   Bb   G   Eb   Bb Ab G F Eb
Num: 1 1 1 2 3   3 2 3 4 5   1   5   3   1   5 4 3 2 1
Solfege: D D D R M   M R M F S   D   S   M   D   S F M R D

USING KEY SIGNATURE

Key of Eb

247

Keys and Key Signature Answer Key *(cont.)*

Start on D, use a key signature or write note for note.

Letters: D D D E E♭ E♭ E♭ G A   D   A   E♭   D   A G F♭ E D .

Num: 1 1 1 2 3   3 2 3 4 5   1   5   3   1   5 4 3 2 1

Solfege: D D D R M   M R M F S   D   S   M   D   S F M R D

Key of ___D___

Start on A, use a key signature or write note for note.

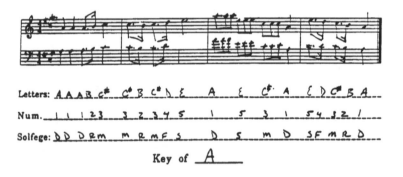

Letters: A A A B C♯   C♯ B C♯ D E   A   E   C♯   A   E D C♯ B A

Num: 1 1 1 2 3   3 2 3 4 5   1   5   3   1   5 4 3 2 1

Solfege: D D D R m   m R m F S   D   S   m   D   S F m R D

Key of ___A___

Part two:

Letters: Ab A♭ A♭ F   G A♭ B♭   A♭ A♭ B♭ A♭ F F.   E♭ A♭ D♭.

Num: 5 5 6 5 3   4 5 6   5 5 6 5 3 3   2 5 1

Solfege: S S L S · m   F S L   S S L S m m   R S D

Key of ___D♭___

Part three: Answers will vary

Basic Playing Technique for Winds and Percussion

Game objectives: To encourage proper breathing, embouchure and intonation for winds; proper stick position, pitch memory and timpani tuning for percussion.

Advance preparation: At the front of the room prepare three "stations of activity:"

Station One. WINDS—a textbook to be placed lengthwise between the chalkboard and a student's abdomen. PERCUSSION—a practice pad and metronome.

Station Two. WINDS AND PERCUSSION—a keyboard, tuner, or pitchpipe that can generate a concert F, A, C♯ and B♭.

Station Three. WINDS—a tuning meter. PERCUSSION—a 28″ timpani and mallet.

All wind players need their instruments, and percussionists need snare drum sticks. Have a stopwatch and prepare a prize for the winning team.

Concept statements:

1. Playing a wind instrument requires proper breathing, embouchure, and tuning skills.

2. Proper breathing requires that the air fill the lungs completely and consequently force the diaphragm to stretch downward and displace the abdomen outward.

3. Proper embouchure allows a brass player to buzz the lips on a specific pitch and then produce a quality tone as he buzzes the pitch into a mouthpiece and finally into the correct length of instrument tubing. Lips "set" for the pitch of A, cause a fuzzy tone when added to the tube length of a B.

4. Proper embouchure control allows a flutist to play two pitches an octave apart on an open headjoint.

5. Proper embouchure produces a shrill concert A on the saxophone mouthpiece and concert C♯ on the clarinet mouthpiece. Correct bassoon and oboe embouchures are required to get the double reeds to vibrate at all.

6. Playing percussion requires proper stick position, pitch memory, and timpani tuning skills.

7. Snare sticks should be gripped between the thumb and index finger at the fulcrum. Palms face down and stick tips should be together. Soft strokes originate two or three inches above the drum head. Loud strokes originate five or six inches above the drum head. Because the flam rudiment requires a stroke at both dynamic levels, it is an excellent check of proper stick placement and control.

8. In order to tune a timpani, the percussionist must be able to hum a reference pitch "into" the timpani and adjust the tuning pedal until the head vibrates with the pitch being hummed.

Game instructions:

1. Divide the class into two teams and instruct team members to arrange their chairs in two single file lines. The game is a relay—each student racing against the time of the student across from him in line.

2. Select one student to go first. At the word go, start the stopwatch and the student begins to work his way through the three stations:

   Station One. WINDS—Lean against the textbook placed lengthwise between the chalkboard and your abdomen. Breathe deeply, and *imagine* the incoming air filling your abdomen and stretching it outwards. As the abdomen expands, you will be pushed away from the chalkboard. As you control the exhale, you will move back toward the chalkboard without dropping the book. Do ten correct sequences of inhale/exhale. PERCUSSION—Play eight 4/4 measures of eighth-note flams at a tempo of 80 beats per minute.

   Station Two. BRASS—buzz a concert F, then maintain the concert F as you buzz the mouthpiece and finally, maintain the F while you slip the mouthpiece into an open horn. SAXOPHONE—produce a concert A on your mouthpiece. CLARINET—produce a concert C♯ on your mouthpiece. OBOE and BASSOON—"crow" the double reed and try to alter the pitch one half-step. FLUTE—produce a concert G on the open headjoint and alter the air stream to produce the concert G an octave higher or lower. PERCUSSION—hum a concert B♭.

   Station Three. WINDS—produce a concert F and adjust your instrument's tube length to the tuning meter. PERCUSSION—hum the B♭ into the timpani and adjust the tuning pedal until the head "sings" back to you.

3. Record the first student's time and start the first student from the second team. The fastest of the two students' times earns 1 point for his team.

4. Continue the relay, comparing the times of each pair, one at a time. The team with the most points at the end wins the game.

General Music and Notation

Game objective: To challenge students' memories while testing their knowledge of musical elements and notation. Individuals strive to gain points by matching cards to make pairs.

Advance preparation: Number each of 40 cards from one to 40. Prepare the back side of each card according to the following diagram—(letter size cardstock paper is recommended):

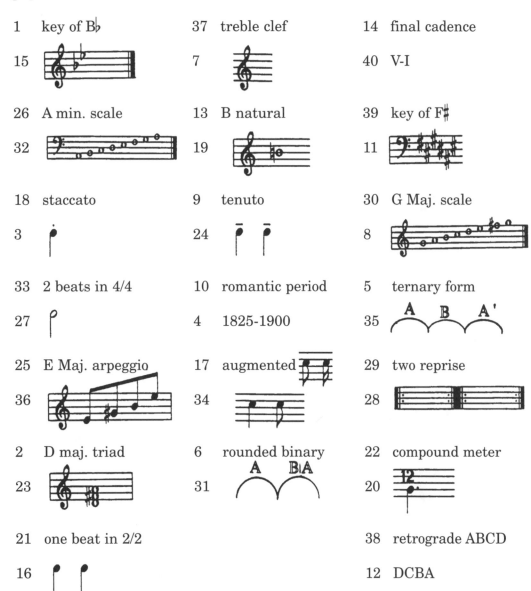

1   key of B♭

15   [musical staff notation]

37   treble clef

7   [musical staff notation]

14   final cadence

40   V-I

26   A min. scale

32   [musical staff notation]

13   B natural

19   [musical staff notation]

39   key of F♯

11   [musical staff notation]

18   staccato

3   [musical note]

9   tenuto

24   [musical notes]

30   G Maj. scale

8   [musical staff notation]

33   2 beats in 4/4

27   [musical note]

10   romantic period

4   1825–1900

5   ternary form

35   A B A' [diagram]

25   E Maj. arpeggio

36   [musical staff notation]

17   augmented

34   [musical staff notation]

29   two reprise

28   [musical notation]

2   D maj. triad

23   [musical staff notation]

6   rounded binary
     A   B|A [diagram]

31   [diagram]

22   compound meter

20   [musical staff notation]

21   one beat in 2/2

16   [musical notes]

38   retrograde ABCD

12   DCBA

Arrange cards numerically in rows of ten across and four down. (Cards should be face down and numbers up.)

251

Game instructions:

1. Have the students sit in a large circle around the rows of cards.

2. One at a time around the circle, each student will choose a card and it will be turned over so that everyone can see the information on its face. The student will select another card in an attempt to match information from one with the other. If a match is made, the student is given both cards and gets another turn. If the cards do not match, both are turned face down again and the turn moves to the next student.

3. When all the cards have been matched, the student with the most pairs wins.

Style Periods and Musical Terms

Game objective: To give students experience with musical terms, definitions, and style periods by way of a fun game called "CLASSWORD."

Advance preparation: Write each of the following words—"CLASSWORDS"—on two separate 5x7 cards. (Each of two teams will need a separate stack.) Organize the two sets of cards according to difficulty level as indicated. Prepare four chairs at the front of the room, one pair of chairs facing each other for each team. Prepare a prize for the winning team.

EASY	MEDIUM	DIFFICULT
Medieval	serialism	alberti
stretto	meter	fugue
ritardando	ethos	ragtime
bridge	aleatory	motif
retrograde	overture	polyphony
Romantic	chant	Expressionism
ternary	key	syllabic
accelerando	chromaticism	exposition
Classical	inversion	enlightenment
binary	responsorial	melismatic
transition	tone-row	Impressionism
Renaissance	suite	ostinato
cadence	modulation	minor

Game instructions:

1. Divide the class into two teams and have two members of each team come to the front. Designate one of the students from each team as the GIVER, and one of the students from each team as the RECEIVER. GIVERS sit on the left chair of each set, RECEIVERS sit on right chair of each set—the GIVER of team one should be back to back with the RECEIVER of team number two.

2. Give the top card from the *easy* stack to GIVER of each pair. *Both GIVERS should have a card with the same word printed on it*. The GIVERS look at the CLASSWORD, but at this point say nothing to their RECEIVERS.

3. After a moment of planning, the GIVER from team number one offers his partner a *one word clue* about the CLASSWORD he has on his card. The clue word cannot be any form of the CLASSWORD or the round is forfeited—a new pair comes to the front and a new CLASSWORD is given.

4. The RECEIVER from team one offers *a one word* guess of the CLASS-WORD. If he is correct, the team is awarded points according to the score chart (below), and the pairs are replaced by new partners who will compete with a CLASSWORD from the *medium* stack. If the guess is incorrect, the procedure of clue and guess moves to the pair from team two. Clues and guesses continue until one of the RECEIVERS guesses the CLASSWORD, or until a total of four clues have been given, at which point the CLASSWORD is announced to all students and the competing pairs return to their seats.

5. The CLASSWORD comes from the *medium* stack only after the *easy* CLASSWORD has been guessed, and so on.

6. The team with the most points at the end of game wins.

SCORE CHART
LEVELS   *Clues and Points Awarded*

Easy	1st clue 20 pts.	2nd clue 15 pts.	3rd clue 10 pts.	4th clue 5 pts.
Medium	1st clue 25 pts.	2nd clue 20 pts.	3rd clue 15 pts.	4th clue 10 pts.
Difficult	1st clue 50 pts.	2nd clue 40 pts.	3rd clue 30 pts.	4th clue 20 pts.

Appendix 2

SAMPLE CHORD PROGRESSIONS

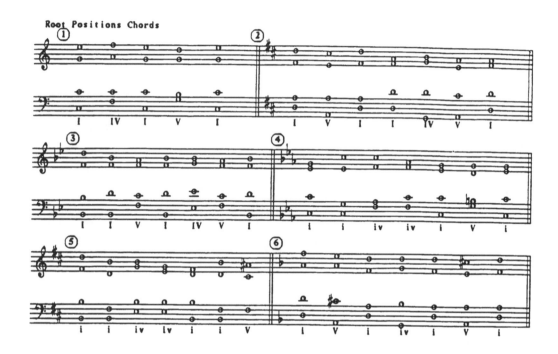

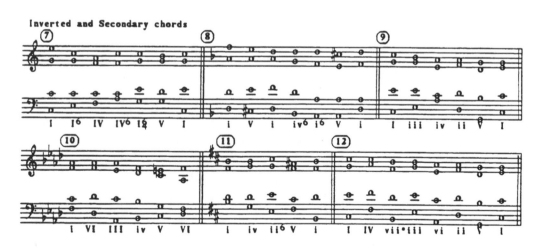

Appendix 3

BAND COMPOSITION TITLES BY STYLE PERIOD

Renaissance

Composer / Arranger	Title	Publisher	Recording
Byrd (1543-1623)/ Jacob (1923)	William Byrd Suite	Boosey	Mercury Record Production Inc.- SRI-75028
Gabrieli (1557-1612)	Canzon Duodecimi Tone	King	
Farnaby (1560-1640)/ Jacob	Giles Farnaby Suite	Boosey	Crest Records- MID-7014
Frescobaldi (1583- 1643)/Slocum	Toccata	Belwin Mills	Crest Records CBDNA-73-1

Baroque

Bach (1685-1750)/ Reed	Jesu, Joy of Man's Desiring	Barnhouse	University of Illinois-53
Bach/Moehlmann	Prelude and Fugue in B♭ minor	Fitzsimmons	
Bach/Holst	Fugue a la Gigue	Boosey	Crest Records- MID-72-5
Bach/Leiden	Toccata and Fugue in C minor	Schirmer	Crest Records- ABA-74-4
Handel (1685-1759)/ Baines and MacKerras	Royal Fireworks Music	Oxford	University of Illinois-46
Handel/Harty	Water Music Suite	Chappell	Mercury Record Production Inc.- 75005
Handel/Phillips	Passacaglia in G minor	Oxford	

Classical
Transcriptions and Arrangements

Composer/Arranger	Title	Publisher	Recording
Beethoven/Hindsley	Egmont Overture	Hindsley	University of Illinois-57
Beethoven/Schafer	Wellington's Victory	Belwin-Mills	
Haydn/Schaefer	Three English Marches	Highland	
Haydn/Duthoit	Trumpet Concerto	Chappell	University of Illinois-23
Mozart/Schaefer	Fantasia in F	Shawnee	Crest Records-ABA-72-4
Mozart/Slocum	Marriage of Figaro	Mills	Crest Records-MID-74-7

Romantic
Original Works

Berlioz (1803-1869)	Symphony for Band Funebre and Triomphale	Schirmer	
Dvorak (1841-1904)	Serenade in d minor, op. 44	Kalmus	
Gounod (1818-1993)	Petite Symphony	International	
Strauss (1864-1949)	Serenade, Op. 7	International	Mercury Record Productions Inc.-90173
Strauss	Suite in B♭, Op. 4	Universal	
Wagner (1813-1883)	Huldigungsmarsch	Shawnee	Crest Records-CBD-69-2
Wagner	Trauersinfonie	AMP	Decca Record Co.-8633
Rossini (1792-1868)	Scherzo for Band	Marks	Crest Records-MID-78-13

Classical
Original Works

Composer / Arranger	Title	Publisher	Recording
Beethoven (1770-1827)	Octet, Op. 103	Breitkopf	
Beethoven	Rondino, WoO 25	Breitkopf	
Beethoven	Sextet	Breitkopf	
Haydn (1732-1809)	Divertimento in F		Mace Records-5-9087
Haydn	Feldpartie in E♭		
Mozart (1756-1791)	Divertimento in B♭, K. 159♭	Breitkopf	
Mozart	Serenade #10 in B♭ K. 361	Breitkopf	
Mozart	Serenade #11 in E♭, K. 375	Breitkopf	
Mozart	Serenade #12 in C, K. 388	Breitkopf	
Mozart	The Abduction From Seraglio	Breitkopf	
Gossec (1734-1829)/ Goldman	Classic Overture in C	Presser	Decca Record Co., Lt.-78633
Gossec/Goldman	Military Symphony in F		

Romantic
Transcriptions and Arrangements

Composer / Arranger	Title	Publisher	Recording
Berlioz (1803-1869)/ Leidzen	March to the Scaffold	Fischer	
Brahms (1833-1897)/ Buehlman	Blessed Are They-German Requiem	Ludwig	
Dvorak (1841-1894)/ Balent	Two Slavonic Dances	Shawnee	
Elgar/Reed	Severn Suite	Sam Fox	

Romantic
Transcriptions and Arrangements
(continued)

Composer/Arranger	Title	Publisher	Recording
Liszt (1811-1886)/ Duthoit	Les Preludes	Podium Music	University of Illinois-48
Mahler (1860-1911)/ Reynolds	Symphony No. 3, Finale	Shawnee	Crest Records MENC-78-18
Moussorgsky (1839-1881)/Leidzen	Pictures at an Exhibition	Fischer	University of Illinois-47
Moussorgsky/Leidzen	Coronation Scene		Crest Records-CBD-69-4
Rimsky-Korsakov (1844-1908)/Leidzen	Procession of the Nobles	Fischer	Crest Records-MID-77-7
Rossini (1792-1868)/ Duthoit	Barber of Seville	Boosey	Capitol Records-535890
Saint-Saens (1835-1868)/ Slocum	Symphony No. 3, Finale	TRN	Crest Records-MID-75-6
Suppe (1819-1895)/ Fillmore	Light Cavalry Overture	Fischer	
Tchaikovsky (1840-1893)/Lake	1812 Overture	Fischer	Crest Records-MID-68-13
Verdi (1813-1901)/ Mollenhauer	Manzoni Requiem Excerpts	Belwin	Crest Records-4035
Wagner (1813-1883)/ Calliet	Elsa's Procession	Warner Bros.	Crest Records-MID-72-8
Wagner/Bainum	Liebstod	Kjos	Crest Records-MID-74-8
Wagner/Hindsley	Flying Dutchman	Hindsley	
Weber/Lake	Oberon Overture	Fischer	

Twentieth Century
Original Works

Composer/Arranger	Title	Publisher	Recording
Amram (1930-)	King Lear Variations	Peters	
Barber (1910-1981)	Commando March	Schirmer	Telarc Records-DG-10043
Bennett, R. (1894-1984)	Suite of Old American Dances	Chappell	University of Illinois-35
Copland (1900-)	Emblems	Boosey	University of Illinois-42
Copland	Outdoor Overture	Boosey	Vanguard Recording Studio-2115-S-348
Copland	Fanfare for the Common Man	Boosey	Columbia Recording Studio-M-30649
Giannini (1903-1966)	Fantasia for Band	Colombo	University of Illinois-42
Giannini	Praeludium and Allegro	Ricordi	Golden Crest Records, Inc.-50084
Gould (1913-)	Jericho	Belwin	
Grainger (1882-1961)	Lincolnshire Posy	Schirmer	
Grainger	Ye Banks and Baes O' Bonnie Doon	Fischer	Crest Records MI
Hindemith (1895-1963)	Konzertmusick, Op. 41	Schott	University of Michigan Band-SM-003
Husa (1921-)	Music for Prague 1968	AMP	Crest Records-4134
Persichetti (1915-)	Divertimento for Band	Presser	Mercury Records-75086
Pisto (1894-1976)	Tunbridge Fair	Boosey	Mercury Records-50079
Schoenberg (1874-1951)	Theme and Variations, Op. 43a	Schirmer	Crest Records-1000
Schuller (1925-)	Meditation	AMP	Northern Illinois University

Twentieth Century
Original Works
(continued)

Composer/Arranger	Title	Publisher	Recording
Stravinsky (1882-1971)	Symphonies of Wind Instruments	Boosey	London Records-6225
Holst (1874-1934)	First Suite in E-Flat	Boosey	Telarc Records-5038
Jacob (1895-1983)	An Original Suite	Boosey	Crest Records-CBDNA-77-2
Vaughan Williams (1872-1958)	English Folk Song Suite	Boosey	Mercury Records-GI-SRI-75011
Walton (1902-1983)/ Duthoit	Crown Imperial	Boosey	Mercury Records-SRI-75028
Bilik (1933-)	American Civil War Fantasy	Southern	Vanguard Records-2124
Chance (1932-1972)	Blue Lake Overture	Boosey	Crest Records-ABA-73-2
Creston (1906-)	Legend	Leeds	University of Nebraska Bands-5
Dello Joio (1913-)	Scenes From the Louvre	Marks	Belwin Mills-104
Grundman (1913-)	American Folk Rhapsody No. 2	Boosey	Boosey & Hawkes
Jenkins (1928-)	American Overture for Band	Presser	University of Illinois-48
McBeth (1933-)	Kaddish	Southern	Southern-McBeth-V-2
Nelhybel (1919-)	Symphonic Movement	Belwin	Crest Records-CBDNA-73-4
Nixon (1921-)	Elegy, Fanfare and March	Fischer	Crest Records-MID-68-8
Reed	Russian Christmas Music	Sam Fox	Crest Records-CRE-9002

Twentieth Century
Transcriptions and Arrangements

Composer/Arranger	Title	Publisher	Recording
Kabalevsky (1904-)/ Beeler	Colas Breugnon Overture	Shawnee	Crest Records-S-4077
Respighi (1879-1936)/ Duker	Pines of Rome	Belwin Mills	Crest Records-CBDNA
Shostakovich (1906-1975)/ Righter	Symphony No. 5, Finale	Boosey	Crest Records-MID-70-5

Twentieth Century
Modern Compositions

Composer/Arranger	Title	Publisher	Recording
Badings (1907-)	Transitions	Shawnee	Crest Records-CBDNA-73-8
Bielawa (1930-)	Spectrum Band/Tape	Volkwein	Belwin Mills-106
Husa (1929-)	Apotheosis of Thie Earth	AMP	Crests Records-S-4134
Mailman (1932-)	Geometrics No. 1	Southern	Crest Records-ATH-5056
Reed, H. O. (1910-)	For the Unfortunate	Kjos	Mercury Records-1138

---

*This table is by no means exhaustive. For additional titles and more complete information including program notes, additional recordings, performance time, difficulty level, and so on, see: Norman Smith and Albert Stoutamire, *Band Music Notes: Composer Information and Program Notes for Over 600 Band Favorites,* Revised Edition (San Diego, Ca. : Kjos West/Neil A. Kjos, Jr., Publisher, 1979).

Appendix 4

BAND COMPOSITION TITLES BY FORM

Binary

Composer/Arranger	Title	Publisher	Recording and Order #
Clifton Williams	Caccia and Chorale	Barnhouse	Crest Records MID-76-10
Clifton Williams	Fanfare and Allegro	Southern	Mercury Records-75094
John Zdechlik	Chorale and Shaker Dance	Kjos Music	Crest Records MID-72-14
John Chance	Incantation and Dance	Boosey and Hawkes	Belwin Mills-102

Ternary

Composer/Arranger	Title	Publisher	Recording and Order #
Robert Jager	Sinfonia Noblissima	Elkan-Vogel	Crest Records MID-68-7
Morton Gould	Ballad for Band	Schirmer	Crest Records-NCBDNA-78-2
Mozart	Fantasia in F	Shawnee	Crest Records-ABA-72-4
Paul Whear	Jedermann	Ludwig Music	
Ingolf Dahl	Sinfonietta mvt. 3	Broude Bros.	Decca-719163
Robert Jager	Symphony No. 1 for Band mvt. 1	Volkwein Bros.	Crest Records-CBDNA-71-1

Fugue

Composer/Arranger	Title	Publisher	Recording
Alan Hovhaness	Symphony No. 4 mvt. 1	C.F. Peters	Cornell Univ. Band Office-CUWE-3
Bin Kaneda	Passacaglia for Symphonic Band	Ongaku-No-Tomo-Sha	Japan Columbia
Bach/Holst	Fugue a la Gigue	Boosey and Hawkes	Crest Records MID-72-5
Bach/Leidzen	Jesu, Joy of Man's Desiring	Carl Fisher	Univ. of Illinois-53

Sonata Allegro

Joseph W. Jenkins	American Overture for Band	Presser	University of Illinois-38
Florian Mueller	Concert Overture in G	Bourne	Crest Records MID-73-7
Vincent Persichetti	Symphony for Band mvt. 2	Elkan-Vogel	Crest Records-NEC-103
Frank Bencriscutto	Lyric Dance	Shawnee	Mark Educational Recordings-2228
Clifton Williams	Dedicatory Overture	Edward Marks Music	Coronet Instructional Media-955
Joseph W. Jenkins	Tocatta for Winds op. 104	Hal Leonard	Crest Records MID-78-8

Rondo

Walter Piston	Tunbridge Fair	Boosey and Hawkes	Mercury Records-50079
Robert Jager	Third Suite mvt. 3	Volkwein	Crest Records-CBDNA-71-7
Vincent Persichetti	Symphony for Band mvt. 4	Elkan-Vogel	Musicians Publications-75086
Jan Meyerowitz	Three Comments on War mvt. 3	Morehead State University Store	

Rondo
(continued)

Composer/Arranger	Title	Publisher	Recording
Holst	Second Suite in F mvt. 1	Boosey Hawkes	University of Illinois-24
Frank Erickson	Balladair	Bourne	Tennessee Tech University Band-Golden Gate

Sectional Variation

John B. Chance	Variations on a Korean Folk Song	Boosey & Hawkes	Crest Records MID-76-7
Robert Jager	Diamond Variations	Volkwein Bros.	Belwin Mills-125
Aaron Copland	Variations on a Shaker Melody	Boosey & Hawkes	Cornell University Band Office-6
Edward Elgar	Enigma Variations	Shawnee	Crest Records-ABA-75-2
Paul Whear	Wycliffe Variations	Ludwig Publications	Crest Records-MID-69-8
John Zdelchlik	Dance Variations	Kjos Music	Crest Records MID-77-8
Clifton Williams	Variation Overture	Ludwig Publications	

Continuous Variation

Gustav Holst	First suite in E-Flat	Boosey & Hawkes	Telarc Records-5038
Bach/Hunsberger	Passacaglia and Fugue in C	Southern	Crest Records-ABA-74-4

*This table is by no means exhaustive. For additional titles and more complete information including program notes, additional recordings, performance time, difficulty level, and so on, see: Norman Smith and Albert Stoutamire, *Band Music Notes: Composer Information and Program Notes for Over 600 Band Favorites,* Revised Edition (San Diego, Ca. : Kjos West/Neil A. Kjos, Jr., Publisher, 1979).

BIBLIOGRAPHY

American School Band Directors Association. *The ASBDA Curriculum Guide (A Reference Book for Band Directors)*. Pittsburg: Volkwein Bros., Inc., 1973.

Bowman, Judith. "Bridging the Gap: Preparing Students for College Music Theory." *Music Educators Journal* 73 (April 1987): 49-52.

Brick, Samuel E. "Teach Discrimination! (A Study of Music Literature)." *Music Journal* 20 (May 1962): 34, 66.

Cogan, Robert and Pozzi Escot. *Sonic Design: The Nature of Sound and Music.* Upper Saddle River, N. J.: Prentice-Hall, 1976.

Cutietta, Robert. "'Performance' Isn't a Dirty Word." *Music Educators Journal* 73 (Sept. 1986): 18-22.

Fowler, Charles, ed. *Sing*. Chapel Hill: Hinshaw Music, Inc., 1988.

Gatlin, F. Nathaniel. "I Don't Know Music." *The School Musician, Director and Teacher* 42 (Aug./Sept. 1970): 74-75.

Garofalo, Robert. *Blueprint for Band*. Fort Lauderdale: Meredith Music Publication, 1986.

Grout, Donald J. *A History of Western Music*. 3d ed. New York: W. W. Norton & Company, Inc., 1980.

Hawaii Music Program, Curriculum Research and Development Group, College of Education, University of Hawaii. *Comprehensive Musicianship Through Band Performance* Zone 4 Book A by Brent Heisenger. Menlo Park, CA.: Addison-Wesley Publishing Company, 1973.

Henry, Earl, and James Mobberley. *Musicianship: Ear Training, Rhythmic Reading and Sight Singing* 1. Upper Saddle River, N. J.: Prentice-Hall, 1986.

Holvic, K. M. "Are We Teaching Technicians or Musicians?" *The School Musician* 23 (Apr. 1952): 12.

[Parker, Kenneth C.]. *What Everyone Should Know About Brass Instruments*. Scriptographic Booklets. Greenfield Mass.: Channing L. Bete Co., Inc., 1966.

Pearce, Wesley. "Intonation and Factors Influencing its Attainment with Special Reference to the School Band." M. A. Thesis, Brigham Young University, 1945.

Peters, Charles S. and Paul Yoder. *Beginning Theory Workbook* Book 1, Master Theory Series. Park Ridge, Ill.: Neil A. Kjos Music Company, 1963.

_____. *Intermediate Theory Workbook* Book 2, Master Theory Workbook Series. Park Ridge, Ill.: Neil A. Kjos Music Company, 1964.

_____. *Advance Theory Workbook* Book 3, Master Theory Workbook Series. Park Ridge, Ill.: Neil A. Kjos Music Company, 1965.

_____. *Elementary Harmony and Arranging Workbook* Book 4, Master Theory Workbook Series. Park Ridge, Ill.: Neil A. Kjos Music Company, 1966.

_____. *Intermediate Harmony and Arranging Workbook* Book 5, Master Theory Workbook Series. Park Ridge, Ill.: Neil A. Kjos Music Company, 1967.

_____. *Advanced Harmony and Arranging Workbook* Book 6, Master Theory Workbook Series. Park Ridge, Ill.: Neil A. Kjos Music Company, 1968.

Randel, Don M. comp., *Harvard Concise Dictionary of Music*. Cambridge: The Belknap Press of Harvard University Press, 1978.

Reed, Owen H. *A Workbook in the Fundamentals of Music*. Melville, N.Y.: Belwin Mills, 1947.

Reid, Robert. *Understanding Music*. Portland: J. Weston Walch, Publisher, 1972.

Reimer, Bennett. "Performance and Aesthetic Sensitivity," *Music Educators Journal* 54 (Mar. 1968): 27-29.

_____. *A Philosophy of Music Education*. Contemporary Perspectives in Music Education Series. Upper Saddle River, N. J.: Prentice-Hall, 1970.

Smith, Larry. "Modern Harmony." Unpublished Workbook for Music Theory Classes, Utah State University, Logan Utah.

Smith, Norman and Albert Stoutmire, eds. *Band Music Notes: Composer Information and Program Notes for Over 600 Band Favorites,* Revised Edition, San Diego: Kjos West/Neil A. Kjos, Jr., 1977.

Spellman, Leslie P. "Neglected Aspects of Music Teaching." *American Music Teacher* 17 (Feb./Mar. 1968): 35, 44.

Stevenson, John R., and Marjorie S. Porterfield. *Rhythm and Pitch: An Integrated Approach to Sightsinging*. Upper Saddle River, N. J.: Prentice-Hall, 1986.

Work, Robert. "Are You Giving Your Students a Rich Musical Experience in Instrumental Music?" *School Musician, Director, and Teacher* 40 (Aug./Sept. 1969): 84.